_____
TO:

_____
FROM:

_____
DATE:

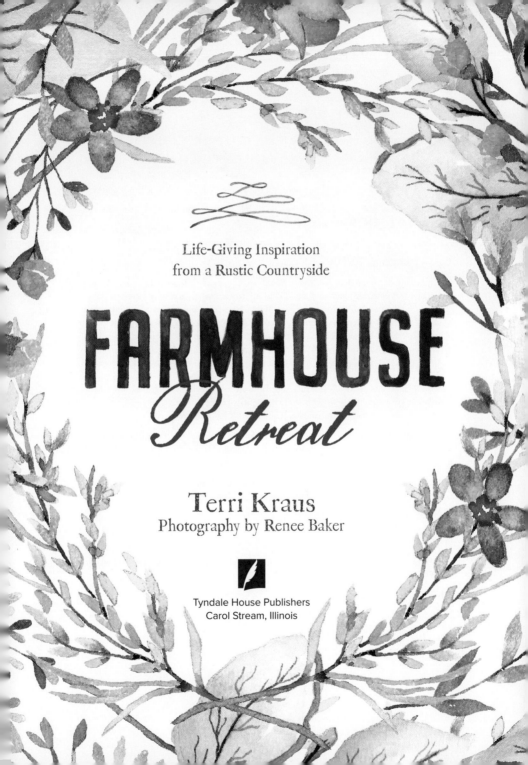

Life-Giving Inspiration
from a Rustic Countryside

FARMHOUSE
Retreat

Terri Kraus
Photography by Renee Baker

Tyndale House Publishers
Carol Stream, Illinois

LIVING EXPRESSIONS COLLECTION

Living Expressions invites you to explore God's Word in a way that is refreshing to the spirit and restorative to the soul.

Visit Tyndale online at tyndale.com.

Visit the author's website at terrikraus.com and the photographer's website at FodderstackFarm.com.

Tyndale, Tyndale's quill logo, *Living Expressions*, and the Living Expressions logo are registered trademarks of Tyndale House Ministries.

Farmhouse Retreat: Life-Giving Inspiration from a Rustic Countryside

Designed by Eva M. Winters

For information about special discounts for bulk purchases, please contact Tyndale House Publishers at csresponse@tyndale.com, or call 1-855-277-9400.

ISBN 978-1-4964-4926-9

Printed in China

27   26   25   24   23   22   21
7   6   5   4   3   2   1

*To my amazing mom—Anna Frances Mascetti, 1924–2017—
my best friend, Italian cook straordinaria, and my most
enthusiastic cheerleader and godliest role model. You taught
me what faithfulness and unconditional love look like.*

Contents

Introduction
Welcome to Fodderstack Farm

FODDERSTACK FARM, a rustic countryside retreat nestled in the western North Carolina mountains, has become one of my favorite getaways since my friends Renee and Drew Baker purchased the property. It's a place where I've enjoyed uniquely connecting with family, friends, myself, and most importantly, God.

Originally called Five Crows Farm, its current name is a nod to nearby Fodderstack Mountain, located adjacent to the Pisgah National Forest, an area with more than five hundred thousand acres of hardwoods, mountainous terrain, majestic waterfalls, white water rivers, and hundreds of miles of trails. The Blue Ridge Parkway, one of America's favorite scenic drives, traverses large parts of the Forest to the northeast and southwest of Asheville—a part of the country breathtaking in its beauty.

Fodderstack Farm is primarily a sheep farm (sometimes called a fiber farm) and is also home to a horse—named Rooster Cogburn after one of the main characters in *True Grit*; two donkeys—Charlotte and Anastasia; chickens; a rooster; ducks; and rabbits. The farm was

started around 1940, the year scratched into a cement block lying in the pasture. The main farmhouse burned down years ago, and the current farmhouse, where the Bakers reside with their dogs and cats, was formerly a cottage for farm workers that they remodeled from the ground up.

The couple who previously owned the farm—the DeVotos—primarily raised goats. With the help of local people, they turned the barn into a house in 1985, retaining its original rustic elements. To maintain the handcrafted feel of the aged barnwood, they used an adze on the beams, giving them a hand-hewn look. The couple enjoyed their retirement on the farm until Mr. DeVoto passed away in 2001 doing what he loved. His ashes were strewn in the back creek in a small ceremony.

Drew and Renee bought the farm in 2013, when Drew left his position as senior manager at a marketing firm in the Chicago area to become a professor at Brevard College. They made more renovations to the barn house, working hard to preserve its historic charm while sensitively blending in many modern updates inside and out. Fencing, multiple structures for the animals, and an off-grid glamping ("glamorous camping") cabin near the creek were added, and they also created a cutting garden. Its flowers and plants provide natural dyes for the yarn Renee spins from sheep's wool, then knits into beautiful works of art. She also creates luxurious soaps and lotions using natural and essential oils.

The Bakers offered their beautifully renovated barn house as a vacation rental for several years, making it the subject of feature articles in *Our State* and *Living the Country Life* magazines. My family and I have been friends with the Bakers since 1986, and we've had the privilege of staying there on several occasions. Each time we visit, rustic warmth and creature comforts enfold us like a loving embrace.

It's our great pleasure to spend time with Drew and Renee while enjoying the animals, mountains, and other charms and serenity the farm offers, but we also delight in exploring the surrounding area. "America's Largest Home," built by George Washington Vanderbilt, sits on the Biltmore Estate, comprised of eight thousand lovely acres that are surrounded by the beauty of the Blue Ridge Mountains. It's a place where nature shouts of God's glory and his astounding creativity.

I have been renewed, restored, and inspired on Fodderstack Farm, where I commune with God in a way that's wonderfully different from my everyday life. It is my deep joy to transport you there and share these blessings with you via my devotions and Renee Baker's amazing gift of photography. My hope is that through the experiences shared in this book, you'll grow deeper in your understanding of our Lord and his loving ways as expressed in his creation and the life of the farm.

His invisible attributes, namely, his eternal power and divine nature, have been clearly perceived, ever since the creation of the world, in the things that have been.

ROMANS 1:20, ESV

For Christ alone—
Terri Kraus

See photos of the farm's history at https://youtu.be/pKgJy2Hr-Ck.

Farm Hospitality

NESTLED AMONG the mountains of southwestern North Carolina, a curving drive leads to Fodderstack Farm, where the gate rests wide open. Just beyond it to the right stands the barn house, where my family and I have stayed as guests. The wide front porch, complete with rockers and a dining table, is adorned with fresh flowers. A lovely floral wreath graces the door, and a small chalkboard beside the door welcomes visitors by name and assures them they are expected with anticipation.

Beyond the entry is the wood-lined and beamed great room, furnished with leather sofas, rustic wood decor, and unique accessories. An enormous antique American flag hangs high on the two-story wall by the staircase. The master bedroom is also wood-lined and beamed; its king-size bed wears a buffalo-check comforter and large, thick shams.

The dining area, with its long farmhouse table and woven rattan chairs, promises wonderful family gatherings. The quaint kitchen features the cabinetry and sink from the original farmhouse, and peeking in the refrigerator reveals a bowl of freshly gathered pastel eggs and other delicious breakfast items.

Upstairs, a loft area provides a cozy place to read, conveniently located between two bedrooms fitted with iron beds covered in quilts. Two comfortable bathrooms offer fluffy towels and luxuriously scented soaps and lotions for the pleasure of each visitor.

The Bakers have thought of everything to make a memorable stay for their guests. The overwhelming feeling and theme of the barn house is *hospitality*, which one source defines as "the friendly and generous reception and entertainment of guests, visitors, or strangers." The word comes from the Latin *hospes*, meaning "sojourner, visitor, guest . . . friend." It's also related to the words *host, hospice, hostel,* and *hotel*.

Hospitality is also a consistent thread woven into the fabric of the Bible's message, presented as a sacred, loving, selfless act of service in which hosts treat family, friends, and strangers alike, warmly welcoming them into their homes and enthusiastically inviting them to share in their lives. In the Old Testament, God commanded his people to extend hospitality to foreigners and sojourners and to love them as they loved themselves—because, he reminded them, they were once exiles in Egypt (Leviticus 19:33-34). The New Testament includes the following commands regarding hospitality:

Offer hospitality to one another without grumbling. Each of you should use whatever gift you have received to serve others, as faithful stewards of God's grace in its various forms.

1 PETER 4:9-10, NIV

Always be eager to practice hospitality.

ROMANS 12:13

Keep on loving each other as brothers and sisters. Don't forget to show hospitality to strangers.

HEBREWS 13:1-2

Most of us know of people in Christian circles who have the gift of hospitality—a serving gift from the Holy Spirit and characterized, we imagine, by one's effortless ability to be "the hostess with the mostest." But ultimately, genuine hospitality is about the heart—about opening one's home and making guests feel welcomed, loved, and cared for, in Jesus' name.

How can you live more hospitably? Think of ways you can open your heart and home to someone who needs a warm welcome.

Morning Dew

IT'S DAYBREAK OVER Fodderstack Farm. The light from the pastel sky pierces through the fog that's hanging over the pasture like a shadowy blanket, illuminating the dew that has settled across the expanse. The moisture condenses on each green blade of grass and each leaf from the trees and plants, forming tiny, shimmering droplets—like miniature diamonds.

It's interesting that the Hebrew word for *dew* appears more than thirty times in the Bible and is frequently portrayed as a gift God sends down from heaven. In the book of Deuteronomy, Moses says,

> Listen, O heavens, and I will speak!
> Hear, O earth, the words that I say!
> Let my teaching fall on you like rain;
> let my speech settle like dew.
> Let my words fall like rain on tender grass,
> like gentle showers on young plants.
> I will proclaim the name of the LORD;

how glorious is our God!
He is the Rock; his deeds are perfect.
　　Everything he does is just and fair.
He is a faithful God who does no wrong;
　　how just and upright he is!

DEUTERONOMY 32:1-4

Moses says that his speech about God's splendor will settle on the Israelites like the morning dew. Even the tiniest droplets of dew don't whisper but *proclaim* (broadcast, announce, trumpet) the glory of God, bringing a drink of morning water to a dry and thirsty land. Though it doesn't make a big show, the dew expresses loudly and clearly the message of God's steadfastness ("He is the Rock") and his perfect deeds, justice, righteousness, and faithfulness.

It may be that we take no notice of such an ordinary occurrence: The dewy landscape presents itself to us in the emerging morning light, beckoning our attention, appreciation, and wonder; but it fails to impact our thoughts and emotions. What if instead we were to train ourselves to pause, pay attention, and let the beauty of a damp morning speak to us?

We see in the verses from Deuteronomy that these gifts of water from heaven are like teachings that fall upon the earth. Moses is begging all of creation to take notice, exclaiming, "Listen, O heavens, and I will speak!" His words point to God's majesty—a miracle happening right before our eyes. And once we see it and learn from it, allowing the miracle to bathe our souls in awe, we can then go forth and proclaim God's glorious attributes.

How many miracles are occurring all around us—not just in the morning but all day long? Are we looking for them and stopping to listen to what they are saying about God, or are we plowing through the hours unaware? It is a matter of intentionality. God is speaking all the time, and we must learn to take notice. Oh, the wonders that we will miss if we don't. Something as ordinary as the dew can become extraordinary when we see God in it.

How can you purpose in your heart to listen for God's voice in the ordinary? Take note of ways he may be showing you his glory throughout your day.

Bird Songs

ONE OF THE LOVELIEST aspects of life at Fodderstack Farm is hearing the songs of the birds in the quietness of the country—especially in the morning. In urban areas, it's easy for the noises of civilization to drown out their melodies. We begin the day by readying ourselves and our families for school and work, and we don't notice the avian choir performing outside.

Have you ever stopped to consider that no matter what the previous day was like, birds always start their new day with a song? When the sun begins to rise, they are already awake and warming up their voices. They live among us, seemingly to provide songs of joy and happiness and bring pleasure to our days.

Bird calls come in thousands of varieties—just a few examples include chirps, whistles, and trills, as well as flutelike, bell-like, and metallic sounds. Most birds have a characteristic tempo, rhythm, pitch, and tone to their calls. Their sounds have different meanings and uses, such as calling to the flock while in flight, contacting or wooing other birds, and, for babies, asking their mothers for food.

A good bird-watcher can tell what species a bird is, sight unseen, just by its call. And yet it's a bird's *song*—which is longer, more elaborate, and includes a string of musical syllables—that is most familiar to us. The melody seems to express happiness and joy.

Isn't it amazing that, like the birds of the air, God, the Creator of the universe, also sings over us? Zephaniah 3:17 says,

> The LORD your God is living among you.
>   He is a mighty savior.
> He will take delight in you with gladness.
>   With his love, he will calm all your fears.
>   He will rejoice over you with joyful songs.

God our Father delights in us and rejoices over us with gladness. He promises to calm our fears. He expresses his love to us like a parent who sings songs of love over their children. Even though we cannot see him, we are able to know him by the sound of his singing as he embraces us—*his* beloved children.

But is this the way we think about God when we come to him? We are often inclined to approach our Father with reservations, realizing how sinful we are, or we approach him seeking something for ourselves or asking for direction. How often do we come to him just to listen for his voice, for how he is singing over us? To delight in his provision of salvation? To pleasure in his favor and unconditional love? He is never too busy to lavish these gifts on us and will not rebuke us or turn us away. Rather, he's waiting for us to quiet ourselves long enough to hear his voice in song—and to relish its beauty and comfort.

Try sitting quietly, eyes closed, imagining that you are in God's arms and he is singing over you. What does his voice sound like? What are the words of his song? Focus on receiving the expression of joy and gladness he has for you. Give him your fears, and allow his song to calm you. Journal what you experience.

Fixer-Upper

THE BAKERS PURCHASED Fodderstack Farm when it was in fore-closure. It had been sadly neglected, with the barn house requiring major updating of electrical, plumbing, heating, and structural systems. Lighting and bath fixtures were replaced, new appliances were added, a large porch was built, and the list continues—just like on HGTV. Now it looks like a rustic Ralph Lauren ad.

There's something about those fixer-upper shows that's magical. The star designer finds a sad-looking place with little redeeming value—dated and tired, ravaged by the years and falling apart. The featured clients arrive and stare in disbelief. "This can't be it," they remark with skepticism. And the designer responds, "All it needs is some love." By seeing its potential and knowing exactly what to demolish and what to repurpose, the designer transforms the property into a dream home.

The designer is a miracle worker. When it's time for the big reveal, the old, rotten, and ugly have all been done away with, and what stands before the clients is fresh and beautiful. The home is completely reborn, ready for new life. There are oohs and aahs, shrieks of surprise and delight, and tears of joy. "This can't be the same house!" the clients exclaim.

Those fixer-upper shows are a beautiful reminder of what Christ does in our lives. Seemingly unredeemable, we come to him weary, world-worn, and in need of perfect love. Our lives may be in tatters—damaged by abuse or ruined by sin, poor choices, or circumstances not of our own making—but Christ sees our great worth. He paid the price for our redemption with his sacrificial death and glorious resurrection. He issues the invitation to abide with him, and when we say yes, he enters in and takes up residence.

By his grace alone, he sweeps us clean of the grime of sin. His love demolishes walls of hard-heartedness, and his mercy permeates the chambers of our hearts that need repair. He restores everything. His Spirit breathes life into the soul, bringing rebirth and new purpose. What seemed hopeless is full of promise.

Just like witnessing the transformation of the Bakers' barn house, it's astounding to see a changed life. It reminds us there is someone—Christ, the true Miracle Worker—who can do this amazing work, and it proves that no one is beyond his power to transform.

Anyone who belongs to Christ has become a new person.
The old life is gone; a new life has begun!
2 CORINTHIANS 5:17

Prayerfully consider those in your life with whom you can share the Good News of Christ's transforming power. Make a list and pray for opportunities. Boost your faith by recalling those whose lives have been changed by our Lord.

Foraging for Decor

Strolling through the woods or along a beach brings freedom and peace to most. Yet despite an innate tendency to seek connections with the great outdoors, people today spend the majority of their time inside, leaving them feeling more disconnected from nature than ever before.

The remedy? Create a happy home that brings the beauty of the outside world in. Surround yourself with plants, natural objects, and images of nature—it's easier than you may think.

Engaging with nature in whatever form, even for a relatively short time, increases our sense of well-being and benefits us physically, spiritually, and emotionally. It reduces our blood pressure, heart rate, and muscle tension; it calms us, reducing feelings of stress, anxiety, and anger; it enhances our mood and stimulates creativity; it makes us feel more compassionate and connected to others and our environment; it improves cognitive performance, focus, and attention; and it even inspires us to be friendlier and more apt to reach out to others in our community.

Although nothing beats immersing ourselves in the true outdoors, we can capture the essence of what nature has to offer with a little creativity and imagination—and without much money.

Foraging is a great way to introduce natural materials like water, wood, stone, clay, branches, shells, nuts, bark, and even weeds into your home. In addition to displaying items in a vase or a bowl, there are many options for decorating your home with nature's visual treasures:

- Flowers, leaves, thistles, fern, moss, and grasses can be tied around a pillar candle or vase, pressed and framed, glued around a mirror, stretched across an embroidery hoop, bundled and hung, made into a wreath, or used as a background in a shadow box.
- Twigs or branches can be arranged in a pot or urn to add vertical height in a corner, or they can be wall-mounted as a sculptural accent or as a means for hanging jewelry, kitchen utensils, linens, or even bags and jackets in an entryway or mudroom. Heavier pieces of wood can be wall-mounted as ledges or shelves.
- Collections of rocks, nuts, bark, shells, feathers, pine cones, and even eggshells can be grouped in a tabletop display (try elevating on a cake plate or under a bell jar) or mounted in a shadow box, suspended on twine, made into a mobile, or used as game pieces.
- Discarded items can even add a bit of rustic chic to your space—think antlers, rusted barbed wire, cans, and glass bottles.
- Although beautiful in their natural state, don't be afraid to add a little drama to your finds with paint, gold, or glitter.

The options are unlimited, so head outside and keep your eyes open to textures, shapes, and colors. Respectfully gather what is interesting, bring it home, and creatively incorporate it into your space. Well-displayed foraged materials add interest and natural beauty to your decor, giving you a sense of calm connectedness to the outdoors and reminding you of God's creativity.

Be Still

SPENDING UNENCUMBERED DAYS on Fodderstack Farm is an open invitation to enjoy time alone in quietness. The farm's private spots beckon one to silence and reflection.

Practicing solitude is also a spiritual discipline that Jesus engaged in; we see in the Gospels how he often withdrew from people, daily activities, and the demands of his ministry to be alone with the Father. He sought a solitary place by going up into the mountains, taking a boat to a remote place, or retreating into the desert.

But for us, spending time in silence and solitude seems counter-cultural. We are constantly bombarded by the demands of work, school, and home for most waking hours of the day, with little opportunity to disengage. We are distracted by television and computers and ever connected to our phones. Because we have everywhere-and-instant access to the internet, social media addiction is real. Getting away from it all and resting in silence is a lost art—and one that some people avoid, perhaps due to the fear of being alone with their thoughts or what God may be telling them.

Yet the practice of silence and solitude has many benefits. From a physiological standpoint, it can lower blood pressure, decrease stress-causing cortisol and adrenaline levels, and boost the immune system and production of brain cells. Psychologically and emotionally, it may help enhance creativity, self-awareness, and the ability to reflect—which goes beyond mere introspection.

Reflection allows us to connect the threads of our disorganized, disconnected world in a way that motivates us to mend strained relationships, change unhealthy habits, or see the possibilities of altering a career path. And from a spiritual standpoint, time spent in reflection allows God to have our uninterrupted attention, as the following Scriptures illustrate: "Be still, and know that I am God!" (Psalm 46:10); "Let all that I am wait quietly before God, for my hope is in him" (Psalm 62:5); "Be still in the presence of the Lord, and wait patiently for him to act" (Psalm 37:7).

My friend, writer and speaker Tina Osterhouse, says, "One of the most significant gifts you can give yourself is time in solitude and quiet. Reflect on the goodness around you, and give thanks. Ask yourself where you are afraid, what makes you feel seen, loved and heard. What is God saying in this moment?"

Reflection requires intentionality. A regular retreat of silence can be just what you need to set aside time for this valuable practice. Whether at a retreat center, out in nature, or on a long hike, drive, or bike ride, we can simply present ourselves before the Lord and ask him to speak.

This prayer from Henri Nouwen can be a helpful start:

Dear Lord, be with me today. Listen to my confusion and help me know how to live it. I don't know the words. I don't know the way. Show me the way. You are a quiet God. Help me to listen to your voice in a noisy world. I want to be with you. I know you are peace. I know you are joy. Help me to be a peaceful and joyful person. These are the fruits of living close to you. Bring me close to you, dear Lord. Amen.

How do the practices of solitude and reflection fit into your life? If you want to be more intentional about spending time alone with the Lord, write a prayer asking for insight on how to make that happen. Then record ideas that come to mind.

Charlotte and Anastasia

TWO DONKEYS LIVE at Fodderstack Farm: Charlotte, a rescue, and her daughter, Anastasia. They are inseparable. These adorable creatures with big ears and observant eyes are gentle, calm, and easygoing.

On a sheep farm, donkeys are also treasured for their heightened defense response, protecting the herd from foxes, dogs, and coyotes. They will stand their ground and chase predators away. Approach the pasture fence and they'll immediately come up to see whether you're friend or foe. Gifted with cautiousness, they have a reason for everything they do.

Donkeys and horses are equine friends. They stick together; when one is sleeping, the other will stay awake to stand watch. Knowing that Charlotte and Anastasia are looking out for him, Rooster Cogburn feels safe to lie down.

Throughout Scripture, God never misses an opportunity to use powerful symbols—donkeys included. One of these gentle beasts of burden carried Mary, pregnant with the Savior of the world, all the way from Nazareth to Bethlehem, an image connecting him with common people. Jesus came to embrace the poor, weak, and oppressed. And in the story he told about the Good Samaritan, the donkey carrying the injured man is a perfect symbol of love and compassion.

Toward the end of his earthly ministry, Jesus arrived in Jerusalem riding on a donkey. Why did the King of Kings choose this animal for his famous Palm Sunday triumphal entry? In the ancient Middle East, leaders rode horses to war but donkeys when they came in peace. Jesus' arrival on what was considered a lowly animal revealed much about his character and great purpose as the Prince of Peace. It also fulfilled a prophecy:

> Look, your king is coming to you.
> He is righteous and victorious,
> yet he is humble, riding on a donkey. . . .
> and your king will bring peace to the nations.
>
> ZECHARIAH 9:9-10

Renee says, "Charlotte and Anastasia, like all donkeys, are deep, loyal, curious, affectionate, intelligent, patient, and protective. They remember everything, so you must be intentional with them. Looking into their eyes and spending quiet time with them is like being with the ancients. To me they are not lowly, but majestic and fitting for a deserving King."

God can use even the humblest of animals for important work on a farm—and to convey Jesus to us as the compassionate, protective, peace-bringing One.

These aspects of Jesus are ones that we should seek to exemplify.
Write a prayer asking God to conform your character more
closely to the image of Christ.

Majestic Mountains

FODDERSTACK MOUNTAIN, elevation 3,015 feet, overlooks the farm. Once the mist clears on a crisp morning, the mountain becomes a beautiful backdrop that dominates the surrounding landscape.

Most of us are captivated by mountains. After all, what's more stunning than a view of snow-capped peaks? What's more striking than the palette of colors created by a mountain sunset or more mesmerizing than the warm hues of their trees in autumn?

We have a sense of wonder about how long mountains have existed and the tectonic forces and volcanic activity that raised them. We stand small in their presence, which helps us put our problems in perspective and sort out what's really important in life.

Besides being enchanting to look at, mountains create spectacular waterfalls, and this area of the Pisgah National Forest, known as the "Land of Waterfalls," is home to more than 250 of them. Mountains also play a significant role in providing nutrition for mankind. More than half of the world's population depends on mountains for water, and mountain pastures feed livestock, which in turn feed people.

Indeed, when God created the world, he knew we needed mountains. His Word uses mountain imagery to convey his character and the nature of his promises. Consider these verses:

I look up to the mountains—
    does my help come from there?
My help comes from the LORD,
    who made heaven and earth!

PSALM 121:1-2

The mountains may move . . .
but even then my faithful love for you will remain."

ISAIAH 54:10

I own the cattle on a thousand hills.
I know every bird on the mountains.

PSALM 50:10-11

The God who spoke the mountains into existence is our Helper and the Creator of all things. Faithful, loving, and merciful, he is worthy of all praise. The whole earth is his, and nature shouts of his glory.

Luke 19:29-40 tells us that when Jesus was coming down the Mount of Olives, riding on a donkey, the crowds threw their garments onto the road ahead of him. They cried, "Blessings on the King who comes in the name of the LORD! Peace in heaven, and glory in highest heaven!" This angered the Pharisees, of course, and they asked Jesus to rebuke his followers for their "blasphemous" praise. Jesus answered, "If they kept quiet, the stones . . . would burst into cheers!"

In Isaiah 55:12, we again see nature rejoicing: "You shall go out with joy, and be led out with peace; the mountains and the hills shall break forth into singing before you" (NKJV).

The stunning beauty of mountains and the wonder they evoke is just one impressive way that God reveals his majesty in nature. If not one person on earth praised him, these enormous pieces of rock are there to give him the glory he deserves. The next time you behold a mountain, think on these things.

Enjoy spending some time writing a prayer of praise, telling God how creation speaks to you of his majesty and glory.

Master Gardener

THERE IS A LOVELY cutting garden at Fodderstack Farm, across the lane from the barn house. Here Renee grows a variety of flowers and plants—some perfect for floral bouquets, and some whose stalks and petals are ideal for making natural dyes to color the yarn she spins from the sheep's wool. Then she knits beautiful garments and throws that perfectly showcase the rich, earthy tones of the dyes. Using her design expertise, she combines the colors in ways that create a unique yet understated impact in each item.

A lot of thought goes into planning a cutting garden. During the winter months, a master gardener decides which varieties of plants and flowers to grow and whether to start them from seeds or potted plants. When deciding their locations, he or she also considers the hours of available sun, the drainage conditions, and how each will look juxtaposed with other flowers and plants.

Achieving a successful and balanced cutting garden requires the persistence of trial-and-error learning. Sometimes plants need to be moved if they are to thrive and enhance the appearance of the whole garden. Creating the best effect depends on taking into account texture, shape, height, spread, and blooming time, as well as the shade of the stalks and the color of the flowers. The goal is to have continuous and varied blooms throughout the growing season so there is always balanced color across the garden. And when at last the planning is finished, the master gardener plants each seed or potted plant in time to benefit from the spring rains. Then the patient waiting begins.

And so it is with us at the beginning of a new season. As the Master Gardener, God considers our unique qualities and purposely plants us, his beloved ones, in specific places for specific reasons. He may decide to keep us where we are or move us to another spot where the conditions are exactly right for us to thrive in his Kingdom. He situates us where we can bring him the most glory.

Jill Briscoe says, "God often uses circumstances to transplant His people into the place He wants them to be." We may question his wisdom in these circumstances, but he knows what he's doing, even when we end up facing difficulties. If we feel we aren't making any headway, we can still trust God to provide what we need to grow in our faith and accomplish his purposes for our lives. He waters us with his Spirit and feeds us with his Word. The light of his love shines on us. All these are given so we can bloom and be fruitful. Be encouraged by Galatians 6:9, which reminds us, "Let's not get tired of doing what is good. At just the right time we will reap a harvest of blessing if we don't give up."

Christine Caine observes, "Sometimes when you're in a dark place you think you've been buried when you've actually been planted." Are you questioning your place right now? Compose a prayer that brings your concerns before God. Ask him to help you trust him, the Master Gardener, to keep placing you where you can bring him the most glory.

Kitchen Herb Garden

How about a sprig of mint to brighten up your tea, fresh parsley to garnish your dinner plate, or maybe a basil pesto to top your steak? Whatever your taste, nothing invigorates a meal like fresh herbs, and no matter the color of your thumb, they can be yours anytime, plucked out of your own garden. Whether it's on a sunny windowsill or a backdoor patio, growing herbs in containers is easy and convenient, saving you money and freshening the air in your home.

To get started, consider whether you would like one big container with multiple herbs, tiered or hanging planters, a wall-mounted arrangement, a window box, or a table with rows of small containers. You may even want to try a hanging pocket garden, fiber grow bags, clay pots, mason jars, or recycled plastic bottles or coffee cans. In addition to garden centers, shop at thrift stores and garage sales, and don't forget to look around your house. Choose a style that coordinates with your decor, or add a personal touch by decorating and labeling your containers.

Next, choose your herbs. Italian herbs such as oregano, basil, parsley, and rosemary are popular options, as are cilantro, sage, and dill. It's much easier to start with seedling plants than straight seeds. Some soft-stemmed herbs—oregano, mint, and basil, for example—do well growing in just water, so if you desire a dirt-free kitchen, you might want to choose one of these.

Otherwise, your next step is to pick up some potting soil, which is lighter than garden soil and ideal for using in containers. Place the soil in your containers, incorporating the seeds or seedlings; then add water and place them in a sunny spot. If you don't have a south-facing window or a location with six-plus hours of sun, you may want to purchase a grow light or full-spectrum bulb.

The care and tending of herbs is as simple as follows:

- Water: Know the moisture preferences of your plants. If you start seeing yellow leaves, you might be overwatering.
- Feed: For healthier plants, use plant food to add nutrients to the soil.
- Prune/Harvest: The more you prune your herbs, the more they grow! Once your plants are at least six inches high or have two to three clusters of leaves, prune them every few weeks. Keep your herbs from flowering to preserve their flavor.

If you don't have a use for all your fresh herbs after pruning, dry them in a dehydrator, tie them together and hang to dry, or place them on a paper towel for a week or so. Store dried leaves in a jar, or freeze the leaves in ice cubes.

Herbs That Grow Well in Containers

If you are cooking . . .	These herbs pair well:
Meat/Poultry	bay leaf, oregano, parsley, rosemary, sage, thyme
Fish	basil, chives, dill, fennel, parsley, rosemary, thyme
Roasted vegetables	basil, dill, fennel, oregano, parsley, rosemary, thyme
Salads/garnish	basil, chives, dill, mint, parsley, lavender, lemon balm,
Beverages	lemon balm, mint, rosemary

If you like . . .	Try cooking with these:
Italian cuisine	basil, bay leaf, oregano, parsley, rosemary, sage, thyme
Mediterranean cuisine	basil, bay leaf, dill, fennel, marjoram, mint, oregano, parsley, rosemary, sage, thyme
Mexican cuisine	cilantro, marjoram, mint, oregano, parsley, thyme
Middle Eastern cuisine	cilantro, dill, mint, oregano
Indian cuisine	bay leaf, basil, chives, cilantro, dill, fennel seeds, parsley, rosemary
Asian cuisine	cilantro, Chinese chives, lemongrass, Thai basil

Come Set a Spell

THE SOUNDTRACK of Fodderstack Farm includes clucking chickens, quacking ducks, bleating sheep, and leaves rustling in the wind. It is a peaceful place to spend time with God. The wide front porch of the barn house, furnished with comfy rocking chairs and boasting a view of the beautiful cutting garden, beckons you to grab a glass of sweet tea and "set a spell" to pray.

Sometimes prayer can seem like a hard discipline; but it can also be a great pleasure. It's easy to vacillate between the extremes: rigid legalism on one end, deeming prayer something that must be checked off our lists, and an unfettered "by the seat of your pants" approach on the other.

God hears all our prayers, of course. We know we should daily confess our sins, remember the needs of others, and pour out our own requests before God, but we often fail to experience the great joy that comes from expressing our praise and thanksgiving. Is there a middle ground where we can both exercise discipline and find joy?

One way to find this balance is to introduce a bit of structure to our prayers. The following acronym, *PRAY*, provides a suggestion for how to shape your prayer time into four topics and includes a supporting Scripture for each one. It weaves the joy of praise and thanksgiving together with the work of confession and supplication—just like Jesus taught us to do in the Lord's Prayer.

P   **PRAISE**

Let all that I am praise the LORD;
with my whole heart, I will praise his holy name.

PSALM 103:1

R   **REPENTANCE**

Now repent of your sins and turn to God, so that your sins may be wiped away.

ACTS 3:19

A   **APPRECIATION**

Be thankful in all circumstances, for this is God's will for you who belong to Christ Jesus.

1 THESSALONIANS 5:18

Y   **YEARNINGS**

Don't worry about anything; instead, pray about everything. Tell God what you need, and thank him for all he has done. Then you will experience God's peace, which exceeds anything we can understand.

PHILIPPIANS 4:6-7

It helps to remember that prayer is a privilege, not a project. Communicating with God is something we *get* to do. And although God is the Creator of the universe, he is the one who knows us completely, sees us clearly, and loves us best. He longs for this intimate relationship and with open arms waits for us to spend time with him.

Whether you're sitting in a porch rocking chair or lounging on the sofa in your living room, time spent in prayer can hold some of the sweetest moments of the day. Enjoy communing with God by writing out a prayer below. You may also want to add your prayers to the journaling prompts at the end of each devotion and record the answers there as well.

Duck House

WE'VE ALL BEEN THERE: It's the middle of the night, dark and quiet. You're supposed to be sleeping, but instead you're plagued with worry, fear, and anxiety. Your thoughts are racing. Problems always seem so much more intense in the stillness of the wee hours. Storms of stress, grief, unforgiveness, resentment, anger, or regret steal away precious hours of needed shut-eye. For a variety of reasons, peace and rest remain far away.

Contrast this scenario with a scene from the idyllic life at Fodderstack Farm, where there is always a rhythm to the day, a routine in caring for the animals. One part of this routine is securing them for the night, ensuring they are safe and where they are supposed to be. When Drew puts his beloved ducks to bed, the darling creatures retreat into their accommodations: a charming little house that is a miniature version of the Bakers' own home on the farm, complete with all the quaint exterior architectural details.

After a day of freely roaming the acres, the ducks begin to gather near the duck house as dusk approaches. Drew then gently directs them toward the door, and they happily waddle inside and wriggle down into their soft hay bed. It is the sweetest thing to experience when, before the lights are turned out and the door is closed, the ducks are "tucked in" by their doting parent with some goodnight words such as, "It looks like we are in for a stormy night. Look after each other, sleep well, and stay safe and warm. I'll see you in the morning."

This brings to mind our heavenly Father, whose watchful care and protection over us is constant—even during those nights when sleep is elusive. It's so comforting to remember these promises from the Bible:

> You can go to bed without fear;
>   you will lie down and sleep soundly.
>
> PROVERBS 3:24

> In peace I will lie down and sleep,
>   for you alone, O LORD, will keep me safe.
>
> PSALM 4:8

> You will keep in perfect peace
>   all who trust in you,
>   all whose thoughts are fixed on you!
>
> ISAIAH 26:3

Envision God speaking these truths over you when you turn out the lights and get into bed. Then pray these comforting words back to him, a powerful experience that can bring you true peace, even in the darkest, stormiest night.

Make a list of the things that are troubling to you, and pray God's peace over each one.

Jesus, King of angels, heaven's light
Hold my hand and keep me through
    this night
FROM "JESUS, KING OF ANGELS,"
BY FERNANDO ORTEGA

Chicken Chapel

AFTER THE DUCKS are put away for the night, it's time to gather the hens into their house, fondly called the Chicken Chapel— a cozy structure with several levels of comfy, straw-lined roosting shelves and gold-framed vintage pictures hanging on the rustic walls.

The hens are beautiful, with each having a unique blend of colored feathers. There is a definite pecking order among them, as evidenced by the order in which they go into the coop. The one at the top gets her preferred nest. The higher a hen roosts, the higher her status, which is sometimes based on when she arrived in the flock. The others follow suit based on their position in the hen hierarchy. When they've all found their spots, Drew gives them his nightly "blessing" as he does with the ducks.

"You're all very special hens, you know," he says tenderly. "Do you know why? Because you each have a name." And he proceeds to say goodnight to each hen: "Goodnight, Little Chicken. Goodnight, Miss Prissy. Goodnight, Grace. Sleep tight, Frankie, Goose, and

Stripey. Sweet dreams, Winona, Dolly, and Smokie." Then he turns out the light and closes the door, the hens all safely inside until morning.

Watching this lovely ritual, one can't help thinking about how God views us as unique, valuable, and worthy of his love. Yet the enemy would love for us to believe we are nobodies—that we are nothing special, unimportant. After all, we know about our personal faults, inadequacies, and missteps, and so often we beat ourselves up for them, imagining that God has no use for us when we are such failures. In the depths of our hearts, we know how far we fall short of God's standards of holiness. We notice others who seem more gifted, good-looking, dynamic, and spiritual, possessing qualities we don't see in ourselves.

But God knows us. He sees us. One popular quote says, "The devil knows your name but calls you by your sin. God knows your sin but calls you by your name." How comforting to know that even in our weaknesses and imperfections, God cherishes us for who we are and has a purpose for each of us.

Tonight when you are drifting off to sleep, imagine God calling you by name and speaking this goodnight blessing over you: "Do not be afraid, for I have ransomed you. I have called you by name; you are mine" (Isaiah 43:1).

Write a prayer thanking God for knowing you, loving you, and treasuring you.

Golf Balls

WHEN THEY ARE about six months old, the Fodderstack Farm chicks have become pullets—young hens—and start to lay eggs. It's important they learn to lay them in the Chicken Chapel's nesting boxes so that Drew and Renee know where to collect them; otherwise the hens would lay eggs all over the farm, attracting marauding foxes and coyotes.

To train the pullets to lay in the proper place, the Bakers place golf balls in the nesting boxes to mimic eggs. When the hens consistently see the balls in the boxes, they learn this is a safe place to lay since the "eggs" are not being stolen by predators.

A pullet disappeared once, and the Bakers assumed she'd been killed. But then she was spotted in a small hay enclosure atop a haystack. The young hen looked dead—until she moved and blinked. Underneath her were twenty-one eggs! This stubborn pullet had placed herself in danger and needed to be retrained.

Sometimes we can be like that headstrong pullet. As we grow in Christ and he shows us his will, his desire is that we stay in the center of it, which is the safest place for us to be. God knows what's best for us. But because we like to run our own lives, we sometimes stubbornly choose to go in a different direction. This penchant to be in control goes back to Adam and Eve in the Garden of Eden:

> The serpent was the shrewdest of all the wild animals the LORD God had made. One day he asked the woman, "Did God really say you must not eat the fruit from any of the trees in the garden?"
>
> "Of course we may eat fruit from the trees in the garden," the woman replied. "It's only the fruit from the tree in the middle of the garden that we are not allowed to eat. God said, 'You must not eat it or even touch it; if you do, you will die.'"
>
> "You won't die!" the serpent replied to the woman. "God knows that your eyes will be opened as soon as you eat it, and you will be like God, knowing both good and evil."
>
> The woman was convinced. She saw that the tree was beautiful and its fruit looked delicious, and she wanted the wisdom it would give her. So she took some of the fruit and ate it. Then she gave some to her husband, who was with her, and he ate it, too.
>
> GENESIS 3:1-6

When presented with the idea that God might not know best, Adam and Eve chose their own desires over God's will for them. And the rest, as they say, is history. In Exodus 32:9, the Lord says of the children of Israel, "I have seen how stubborn and rebellious these people are." Some translations call them "stiff-necked people." God had shown them repeated acts of mercy, patience, and long-suffering, but they hardened their hearts toward his direction in their lives.

As children of Adam and Eve, we are born sinful. Inherent in all of us is the temptation to go our own way. Just like that young hen, we can let our stubbornness put us in danger. Or instead, we can determine in our hearts to obey God's commands and rest in the knowledge that his way is superior to any plan we can devise ourselves.

Are there any areas of your life where God needs to place some golf balls to rein you in from going your own way?

Raising Chickens

What would Old MacDonald's farm be without a *cluck, cluck* here and a *cluck, cluck* there? For centuries, chickens have contributed to culture, art, cuisine, science, and religion. They were first domesticated for cockfighting, but today chickens are raised worldwide for their meat and eggs.

Until the early 1900s, chicken production was mostly a casual, local enterprise, and chickens typically spent their days wandering around the barnyard, pecking for food. But after the development of feed containing vitamins and antibiotics—allowing chickens to be raised indoors—commercial chicken farming boomed. By the early 1990s, chicken had surpassed beef as America's most popular meat.

Yet many Americans have developed a distaste for the crowded facilities and use of antibiotics characteristic of large farming practices. Raising chickens at home has become a growing trend, offering the benefit of healthy, delicious, freshly laid eggs. Chickens can also be raised for meat if you are so inclined.

Keeping chickens does take time and money, but it can be an interesting and enjoyable hobby or source of side income. Although communities are getting behind the trend, you'll first want to confirm it is allowed in your area. Then, as with any new endeavor, you'll need to do your research.

Rather than purchasing mature chickens, most people start with chicks, which can be bought from a local farm or feed store. You can choose from a variety of breeds based on your goals, climate, and preference. Baby chicks require a "brooder" to keep them safe and warm, often simply a cardboard box with a heating appliance that can be kept in your garage or storage area.

For the first few weeks, you'll need to check on them multiple times a day and provide them with fresh food and water and clean bedding. When the chicks are about six weeks old, they should be ready to graduate to a coop outdoors.

Chicken coops come in all shapes and sizes. Make or buy them as rustic or as ornate as you please. Be sure that the coop is roomy enough and built for your climate, that it protects the chickens from predators, and that it provides access for collecting eggs and cleaning.

If you study up on chicken growth and flock social patterns, feed your birds a well-balanced diet, care for their physical health, and keep their space clean (they poop a lot!), they will reward you each morning with eggs.

Although chickens are not traditional pets, be aware that you may get emotionally attached to your new farm friends and find yourself giving them endearing names, referring to them as "your girls," enhancing their coop, or splurging on other "pet" extras!

Chickens: Did You Know?

- A tissue analysis from T. rex dinosaur bones excavated in Montana in 2003 indicates the dinosaur shares more genetic material with domestic chickens than with reptiles.

- Domestic chickens may have come to the Americas from Polynesia at least one hundred years before Columbus. At an archaeological site in coastal Chile, excavators found chicken bones dated between AD 1304 and 1424.

- Chickens arrived in North America from Europe in the sixteenth and seventeenth centuries when Dutch and Portuguese slave traders brought them over from Africa; chicken remains similar to those found in Spain have also been found in Haiti and Florida.

It All Matters

A VERY IMPORTANT FIGURE associated with Fodderstack Farm is Dr. Vicky, the farm veterinarian. She advises the Bakers on how to care for the animals' health and makes an annual spring visit to deworm and immunize the sheep. If one of the animals gets sick, Dr. Vicky administers the proper medication. If an animal is injured, she comes with her remedies to set a bone or treat a bad cut.

But despite all the measures taken, sometimes the outcome isn't favorable. One example is Red, a New Hampshire Red chicken who was ailing after flies attacked her, causing an infection called flystrike. Dr. Vicky gave Red injections, and the Bakers lovingly nursed her. Yet after much effort, she ended up having to be put down— a sad day at the farm. Sometimes all the valiant medical measures in the world aren't enough to save a creature.

Suffering and death are part of animal life, even on a bucolic farm, and they're the realities of human life as well. Even our most idyllic circumstances are interrupted by hardship and tragedies at times. For both the believer and unbeliever, this is the inescapable truth.

Suffering was not God's original intention; his creation was perfect in the beginning. But from the moment Adam and Eve first sinned in the Garden, the world has been broken, and it will remain so until the day Christ returns and makes all things right.

In the meantime, we seek to avoid the consequences of mankind's rebellion against our Creator. When death is the prognosis for ill loved ones, we may naturally opt for elaborate life support systems to prolong their days. And although medical science pursues treatments that will allow humans to live longer, even it is limited. The giving and taking of life is God's prerogative alone. Psalm 139:16 says, "You saw me before I was born. Every day of my life was recorded in your book. Every moment was laid out before a single day had passed."

God is *sovereign*, with a plan and purpose that are often not understood or obvious to us. But we also know that he is *good*, not just in what he does but also in his character—and he cannot go against it. The Bible tells us, "There is only One who is good" (Matthew 19:17), and "God is light, and there is no darkness in him at all" (1 John 1:5). When we face illness, we must still pray and seek medical help, but always with humility, trusting the outcome to God's will. And although we will suffer and die, Jesus is worth following because he makes even the hard things *matter* for eternity.

Believer: There is great hope! Be assured that your suffering is not meaningless. God's highest goal for you is to become increasingly like Jesus. Your prayer should always be, "Make it count, Lord."

Unbeliever: If you can't make sense of your suffering and you fear death, come to the peace God offers. He is not capricious; he knows what he's doing. And when you belong to him, he redeems your suffering by giving it an eternal purpose.

Write out your thoughts on suffering and death, confessing areas that may not be aligned with a biblical view. Ask God for the peace that comes from knowing he is sovereign and good.

Crow Angels

FODDERSTACK FARM was originally called Five Crows Farm. Drew and Renee discovered why one day when they observed the farm's horse, Rooster Cogburn, standing in a strange position as he stared at a commotion in the pasture. Upon further investigation, the Bakers found a hawk standing among four ducks on the ground while several crows were diving down, trying to attack.

The ducks, being out of their water element, had no natural defenses to guard themselves. They were very frightened and overpowered. If they tried to fly away, they would be caught in the hawk's talons. The situation grew more intense, but after continued attacks by the crows, the hawk finally flew away. The ducks waddled off, and the crows settled on the fence near them. If that group of crows had not intervened to save the ducks, carnage would have ensued.

The threat of predators to farm creatures is always a concern. Sensing danger, chickens usually crouch down and hide when they hear a hawk's cry or see its shadow. Crows are territorial and will guard birds of other species because the same predators could attack

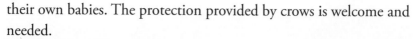
their own babies. The protection provided by crows is welcome and needed.

As humans, we also face "many dangers, toils, and snares." We often feel that we are under attack in a variety of ways. But how amazing to know that instead of dispatching crows, God sends angels to protect us! Angels are celestial beings who act as intermediaries between God and humanity, protecting and guiding and carrying out tasks on behalf of their Creator.

In stark contrast to black farm crows, we usually imagine angels as beautiful winged beings dressed in white cloaks and glowing with a body-engulfing halo. While that may or may not be true, God often sends them as invisible beings or dressed in special clothing that blends in with their surroundings as they perform their assigned duties.

The Bible is full of occasions when God's children experienced the intervention of an angel. How wonderful to think that God loves us so much that he dispatches his angels to minister to us when danger threatens and we are in need of special aid from heaven!

Let the following Scriptures strengthen your faith as you consider how the Lord is able and willing to send you the gift of angelic help.

> The angel of the Lord is a guard;
>   he surrounds and defends all who fear him.

PSALM 34:7

> Angels are only servants—spirits sent to care for people who will inherit salvation.

HEBREWS 1:14

CROW ANGELS

Don't forget to show hospitality to strangers, for some who have done this have entertained angels without realizing it!

HEBREWS 13:2

Can you think of a time when you were sure that angels had protected you or a loved one?

Joy Stones

A LOVELY CREEK RUNS along the far side of the lower pasture at Fodderstack Farm. On its bank is a "glamping" cabin. "Glamorous camping," the meaning of this mash-up word, is a description that fits it to a T.

Constructed of locally harvested and milled live-edge pine siding, the cabin has a spacious screened porch for relaxing and dining, with French doors that connect to a luxurious bedroom. The inviting sleeping space includes a large barn-board bed layered with comfy quilts and lit by a pair of bedside sconces, sheepskins on the wooden floor, a fine mahogany bookcase, and a potbellied stove flanked by elegant chairs. But the nicest feature of this wonderful place is the lovely and relaxing background music the creek provides.

It has been said that a brook that flows over stones makes the sweetest music, and if you remove the stones, the brook will lose its song. This is also true of our personal experiences. We all have "stones" in our lives—trials and afflictions that seem to impede our ability to move through our days untroubled. We want to remove these impediments as quickly as possible and get past them unscathed, hoping we won't run into them again. But James 1:2-4 tells us,

> When troubles of any kind come your way, consider it an opportunity for great joy. For you know that when your faith is tested, your endurance has a chance to grow. So let it grow, for when your endurance is fully developed, you will be perfect and complete, needing nothing.

We view blessings as comfort, ease, and the fulfillment of our desires. But Scripture tells us that we can find blessings in times of difficulty as well. They may not be joyous experiences—suffering is not pleasant—but we are to *consider* them as occasions for "great joy." Why? Because they are necessary to grow our faith, produce Christlikeness, and make us whole and complete. Blessings can thrive as we travel over stones of affliction, and they are often the means by which we see God's faithfulness, love, and power sustain us. We are transformed in ways not possible by any other means.

As we journey through difficulties, we learn to trust God, believing he has a purpose and a plan for them. We can rejoice in these truths by seeing them as the fulfillment of what should be our greatest desire—to be like Jesus. Our passage over those difficult stones can produce beautiful music. The song of joy we choose to sing during these times can testify of our faith to unbelievers and encourage our fellow believers, helping them to see that they, too, can overcome.

Journal a prayer asking God to help you see your stones as ways of becoming more Christlike. Ask him to help you make them count and enable you to sing a song of joy as you pass over them.

Changing Seasons

FODDERSTACK FARM LIFE is very much segmented by the seasons nature provides, with a rhythm to each.

Winter is a time of planning and reflection; life pauses in anticipation. The animals are more dependent on the Bakers since their water freezes over and the ice must be broken up every day. The horse, sheep, and donkeys eat grass down in the three pastures, but it must be supplemented with hay. They love the snow—especially the sheep, who romp and play in it. There's time to plan farm improvements and spin and dye sheep's wool for knitting projects. Fur from the Angora rabbits also lends itself to luxurious yarn.

In spring, tasks change to fertilizing the pastures, cleaning out the barn and outbuildings, and hatching new chicks by putting fertilized eggs under a broody hen. The sheep are sheared, and the animals get checkups and vaccinations. Birds weave nests from Charlotte's and Anastasia's brushed-out hair, and new life emerges everywhere—including adorable lambs and baby chicks.

In summer, the pasture animals eat grass exclusively. Charlotte and

Anastasia wear a muzzle with a small hole to limit their intake; as desert animals, too much grass isn't good for them. At night they're put into the barn unless the coyotes are especially vocal. Sheep tend to sleep more in the hot weather, so Charlotte and Anastasia are called on to protect them when predators are lurking. Thankfully there are few weather concerns that would endanger the animals.

The coming of autumn means preparing for winter and enjoying gorgeous fall colors. The chickens molt their feathers, and Rooster Cogburn and Charlotte and Anastasia get their winter coats. Things quiet down around the farm with more meditative activities like dividing and transplanting flowers and planting young trees. The persimmon tree drops its sweet fruit, and other trees shed their vibrant leaves in anticipation of a long winter sleep. It's time to hand-make luxurious cold-process soap using natural and essential oils. After turning over the cutting garden's soil, next spring's garden is planned.

Just as there are seasons on the farm, there are seasons in our lives too. The Bible describes them in Ecclesiastes 3:1-8:

A time to be born and a time to die.
A time to plant and a time to harvest.
A time to kill and a time to heal.
A time to tear down and a time to build up.
A time to cry and a time to laugh.
A time to grieve and a time to dance.
A time to scatter stones and a time to gather stones.
A time to embrace and a time to turn away.
A time to search and a time to quit searching.

A time to keep and a time to throw away.
A time to tear and a time to mend.
A time to be quiet and a time to speak.
A time to love and a time to hate.
A time for war and a time for peace.

The saying goes that the only constant in life is change. The seasons of life ebb and flow as they do in nature. The challenge is to embrace them as from the hand of our Father, fully experiencing and appreciating them for what we can learn. Resisting these ever-present changes can cause unnecessary pain and suffering, but yielding to them as a vital part of our journey helps us experience more peace and contentment.

Looking back on the seasons of your life, what have you learned from each one?

Old-Time Laundry

No household chore has been around longer than laundry. Ever since women could be seen by the creekside beating their dirty laundry with rocks, the never-ending task of keeping clothes and linens clean has possibly been one of the least favorite the world over.

Before electricity was common, your ancestors likely did laundry by hand, either down by the river, in a tub with a washboard, or in a hand-cranked agitator. These are all still options today, and many homesteaders and off-the-grid pioneers are reviving these nonelectric options.

Our automatic washers and dryers greatly reduce the time and manual labor required, but they also remove us from some of the benefits of how laundry was done in earlier, slower-paced times. Consider recapturing the nostalgia of laundry air-drying on a clothesline, sheets snapping in the breeze—all while reducing your energy bill and enjoying a few minutes outdoors. A simple clothesline strung up in the yard, on the porch, or even in your kitchen or bathroom is all it takes to make this small shift in your laundry routine.

Another back-to-basics switch is to try making your own laundry detergent. It's an affordable option that's free of strong chemicals. A simple web search reveals many recipes that involve mixing two commonly available household products—borax and washing soda—with fine shreds of a bar of laundry soap. Another all-natural method is to mix washing soda, baking soda, and castile soap. Gentle and completely biodegradable, castile soap originally used olive oil as its fat base and is now made with a variety of vegetable-derived oils, including coconut, avocado, walnut, almond, and hemp. Try scenting your recipe with a few drops of your favorite essential oil—lavender, rosemary, tea tree, peppermint, or lemon. There are some concerns about soap scum buildup on clothes and laundry machines with homemade detergent, but much of that can be alleviated by using hot water and adding vinegar in the rinse cycle. You can easily tweak the detergent recipe for the soap balance that works best for your needs and the hardness of your water. You may not be able to avoid having to do laundry, but with a few small changes, you can enjoy using an effective and more natural laundry detergent while reducing costs and energy use. It may not feel as efficient to reintroduce some traditional methods to your process, but if you decide to give them a try, use the moments when you're hanging up those shirts or folding the fresh sheets to be grateful for the options you have—and be glad you didn't need to pound your jeans with a rock!

Washing Machines: Did You Know?

- 1858: The first rotary washing machine was patented, though it was hand–cranked and still a lot of work to use.

- 1908: The first electric washer was developed.

- 1930s: The first fully automatic washer with a spin cycle was marketed.

- In 2016, more than 85% of all US households had a washing machine.

- In 1955, only 10% of US households had a clothes dryer; this figure rose to nearly 80% by 2009.

- In 2006, 83% of Americans considered the clothes dryer a necessary appliance. By 2010, the percentage had dropped to 59% according to a survey by the Pew Research Center.

On Helplessness

IT'S 4:00 P.M. at Fodderstack Farm, and all its creatures—the sheep, horse, donkeys, hens, rooster, ducks, and rabbits—are alert and waiting with anticipation for what happens every day at this hour: mealtime! The treats are the highlight of their day.

It's safe to say that none of the animals go hungry and that they receive lots of love. Drew and Renee meet all their physical needs, making sure they have their daily "bread" and water and providing them with safe shelter and health care.

The Bakers' devotion can be seen in Shelly Webb, an Indian Runner duck, and Inky and Cora, two Bantam mini ducks. Drew and Renee enjoy the thrill of watching the first wiggles of hatching eggs, so all three were hatched in an incubator in their bedroom. Then they raised the ducks in their living room in a big open-top plastic container until they were old enough to go outside safely.

Renee also picks up newborn lambs after they are born and puts them into a lambing "jug"—a small area she prepares with clean straw and fresh water, food, and hay. She also includes a salt block and sheep minerals for the mom, who follows her babes into the jug. Keeping the lambs in this area helps to protect them and ensures they bond with their mom. The jugs are kept well-bedded, dry, and free of drafts. For the first week or so, Renee will put fleece pajamas on the lambs if the temperature dips below forty degrees. She also spends lots of time sitting in the jugs to watch the lambs and allow them to get used to her.

In their helplessness, these fortunate animals do not fight the devoted care they are given, but seem grateful for it. Yet as humans, we view helplessness negatively. We care for our babies when they are newborn and helpless, but once they begin to grow, we expect them to increasingly help themselves and become less and less dependent.

Not so with God. He wants us to realize that our helplessness before him means we're ever dependent on his care. We must keep coming to him in prayer for our very survival as Christians.

These words by Norwegian theologian Ole Hallesby put it well:

Be not anxious because of your helplessness. Above all, do not let it prevent you from praying. Helplessness is the real secret and the impelling power of prayer. You should therefore rather try to thank God for the feeling of helplessness which He has given you. It is one of the greatest gifts which God can impart to us. For it is only when we are helpless that we open our hearts to Jesus and let Him help us in our distress, according to His grace and mercy.

We have no power in this exchange; God has it all, and we come impotent and totally reliant on him to fill us. This is where he wants us; this is being in right relationship with him. John 15:5 says, "Apart from me you can do nothing." And that is a very positive thing.

In what ways are you unable to come to God in the attitude of helplessness? Compose a prayer asking him to help you recondition your heart to depend on him in prayer more and more.

Bluegrass Beauty

EVERY SEPTEMBER, Brevard, North Carolina, the nearest town to Fodderstack Farm, hosts its popular Mountain Song Festival. Thousands gather at the Music Center's open-air venue, nestled into a beautiful cove with the Pisgah National Forest as its backdrop. Local artists pay homage to the area's bluegrass music tradition, which has been woven deeply into the culture and history of the surrounding mountains for generations.

Mountaineering expert and photographer Bob Sihler writes, "Stepping into the Blue Ridge is like stepping into a folk song about a bygone era of bygone values and ways, and the breezes bear the songs of ghostly fiddles and the forgotten people who made them talk and who played a fundamental and lasting role in the development of American culture."

One of the primary themes in bluegrass music is the gospel message of God's saving grace. You will find touchstones to the Christian faith in nearly all bluegrass performers' repertoires. These evocative

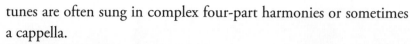

tunes are often sung in complex four-part harmonies or sometimes a cappella.

Bill Monroe, the "Father of Bluegrass," is credited with creating the sound that we've come to know as bluegrass music when his band, the Blue Grass Boys, were pickin' and fiddlin' together in this distinct style in the 1940s. The lyrics of his song "A Voice from On High" reflect the genre's gospel roots. Beginning with "I hear a voice callin', it must be our Lord," they go on to speak simply, yet profoundly, of our heavenly prize—and the great price that was paid for our salvation.

Bluegrass songs often speak of life's struggles and the Christian's eternal life to come. Another example is "Just a Little Talk with Jesus," about a sinner who finds the light of Jesus. It encourages us to talk with the Lord whenever we're troubled—because "he will hear our faintest cry and he will answer by and by."

The Bible is full of verses about singing. Many of the Psalms are the lyrics of David's songs. Ephesians 5:18-19 instructs, "Be filled with the Holy Spirit, singing psalms and hymns and spiritual songs among yourselves, and making music to the Lord in your hearts."

Composer Zoltán Kodály wrote, "There is no complete spiritual life without music, for the human soul has regions which can be illuminated only by music." How wonderful it is that God made us with the ability to express our hearts' joys and laments through the beauty of music—and allows us the pleasure of listening to and appreciating it.

How has music illuminated your soul? Write out the words to your favorite gospel song and thank God for the gift of music.

The Treasure of Time

VISITORS TO FODDERSTACK FARM often say they love unplugging, experiencing unstructured moments that beckon them away from their phones—seeing the chickens greet the morning with pecking and scratching, enjoying the sheep as they graze contentedly, wrapping a shawl around their shoulders and watching the sun dip behind the mountain. Time away from home allows them to take a step back from the tyranny of the urgent, the expected, and the routine.

To function in the world, our lives are geared to focus on how we spend the hours in a day. We anticipate the time it will take to accomplish needed tasks and where we have to be at a certain hour. We're often looking at the clock, not thinking about how the way we use our days adds up in the long run.

Time is indeed precious, and the Bible has much to say about how we spend it:

> Be careful how you live. Don't live like fools, but like those
> who are wise. Make the most of every opportunity in these

evil days. Don't act thoughtlessly, but understand what the Lord wants you to do.

EPHESIANS 5:15-17

How do you know what your life will be like tomorrow? Your life is like the morning fog—it's here a little while, then it's gone.

JAMES 4:14

It is required that those who have been given a trust must prove faithful.

1 CORINTHIANS 4:2, NIV

God has put each of us on this earth to matter significantly. This doesn't mean that we will all become famous for achieving things the world deems important. It means bearing the fruit of the faith we confess, being found faithful in doing what pleases God, and fulfilling our mission to further the gospel. It means being a godly parent or a devoted son, daughter, or grandchild; serving the least and the lost in Jesus' name; reaching out to the lonely and homeless; caring for widows and orphans; and giving our resources to ministries on the front lines of spreading the Good News.

Every day is a treasure God has given us to use for his glory. The things of earth are passing away, and life is short. As good stewards of our time, we must spend it on things that will last forever, to hold on to what will stand in eternity. The words of Henri Nouwen can be a great daily reminder:

Did I offer peace today? Did I bring a smile to someone's face? Did I say words of healing? Did I let go of my anger and resentments? Did I forgive? Did I love? These are the real questions! I must trust that the little bit of love that I sow now will bear many fruits . . . in this world and in the life to come.

One helpful exercise is to view your life as a pie chart. List the major elements where your time is spent each day, week, and month. Then assign them a percentage as slices of a circle. Does anything surprise you? In light of eternity, do you need to make some adjustments? Ask God for his help with this.

Mother Hen

A STAY AT FODDERSTACK FARM often includes the invitation to gather fresh eggs each morning from the Chicken Chapel. The eggs appear in a variety of lovely colors—from pure white to warm cream, sage green to pale pink, baby blue to chocolate brown—and you will never enjoy more intensely "eggy" eggs on your palate than these!

If the hens are nearby when you approach the henhouse, they might show fierceness, instinctively trying to protect their eggs with their lives. Sometimes they may even pretend they are hurt to draw predators away from the nest—a powerful picture of motherly devotion and sacrifice.

The Bible contains many different images of God, including one that is unique and compelling: God as mother hen, fervently wishing to protect her chicks. In Matthew 23:37, Jesus uses this description of himself as he looks out over Jerusalem:

O Jerusalem, Jerusalem, the city that kills the prophets and stones God's messengers! How often I have wanted to gather your children together as a hen protects her chicks beneath her wings, but you wouldn't let me.

In these words, we can see how Jesus *longed* for his people to come to him. His tenderness and loving-kindness were on display. We can hear his frustration at how, time and again, they rejected his love and instead carried on in their own disobedient ways. Based on their behavior, they were seemingly unworthy of this amazing offer, and yet with open arms he wanted to gather them to himself. Just like a mother hen draws her chicks under her wings, he desired to love them, care for them, and protect them. How sad that they were *unwilling*.

What a picture of God's grace—his unmerited favor. Not one of us is a worthy recipient of his love, but we can come to him despite our imperfections, sins, failures, and shortcomings, and his offer stands. He loves us with a fierce love, like a mother hen, drawing us close, where we belong—protected and well cared for by our Creator and Savior.

Are you willing to come to him? Under his wings you will experience perfect comfort and love. Even at your worst, and at the worst of times, you will be covered with the feathers of God. There you will find refuge, safety, and peace.

He will cover you with his feathers.
    He will shelter you with his wings.
    His faithful promises are your armor and protection.

PSALM 91:4

Consider ways in which you are not allowing God to draw you close. Are there areas in your life where you are resisting his love?

Farm-to-Table

Farm-to-table is a relatively new term in trendy dining. It probably amuses farm folks since they have been eating this way for generations! At one time, raising your own food was the normal way of life. But as people moved from rural areas into cities when industrialization ramped up, they became more and more removed from their sources of food.

Farm-to-table means more than just "It came from a farm"—which can be said of most food. It means it came *directly* from the farm and wasn't shipped, processed, frozen, held in a distributor's warehouse, or stocked in a grocery store on its way to your table.

A growing food trend in the US, farm-to-table aims to bring locally grown, nutritious, ethically raised, and often organic food to our plates. Of its many benefits, probably the best one is that your food will taste better. Since locally grown food doesn't need to be transported and processed, it's allowed to mature and ripen in place, creating more flavor and increasing available nutrients.

Economic and environmental benefits include less air pollution and use of pesticides, as well as healthier soil, due in part to crop rotation methods used by many small farms. Buying local food also creates local jobs, positively impacting the community. Your own pocketbook will benefit, too, if you adjust your menu to take advantage of seasonal, readily available meat and produce.

Depending on where you live, it may be hard to become an exclusive "locavore," but the following tips can help shorten the distance between you and your food. Bon appétit!

- Plant an outdoor garden or an indoor herb garden.
- Buy direct from a local producer or at a roadside stand.
- Find a "U-pick" opportunity for a family outing.
- Get to know the vendors at a local farmers market; ask about recipes and cooking tips.
- Join a food co-op, which works with multiple suppliers to provide a variety of fresh, local, and seasonal products at a great price.
- Subscribe to a CSA box. Community Supported Agriculture (CSA) is the term for paying for a share of a farm in exchange for a weekly or biweekly box of fresh produce. Support the farm, and get fresh food directly from the source. Many CSAs will deliver to a drop-off location, making it workable even if you don't live nearby.
- Attend a dinner hosted by a farm. Many farms host fundraisers or plan special dining experiences that allow people to enjoy literal farm-to-table meals in a natural setting, often served family style.
- Eat at a farm-to-table restaurant. Be careful, however, about farm-to-table claims, as there's no standard criteria or regulated definition of the term, and some restaurants may take advantage of the buzzword without actually using local ingredients. Anyone using the phrase "farm-to-table" should serve what is in season in your area and be forthcoming about the local farm or supplier where their food comes from.
- Consult localharvest.org or other online resources for information about local farms, farm stands, farmers markets, CSAs, and farm-to-table restaurants.

Healing Balm

ONE OF THE PLEASURES of staying in the barn house at Fodderstack Farm is the opportunity to indulge in the luxury of Renee's handmade soaps and lotions. These lovely, extra-creamy balms exude wonderful earthy scents of lavender, mint, rosemary, and rose. Soothing and comforting, they fill the senses and dissipate aches.

But is there a balm for the soul—one that can give us the care we need to soothe our internal pain? In the depths of our being, isn't that what we all desire? When life turns hard, we need to find relief amid our suffering, sorrows, and losses.

It's impossible to watch the news or scroll through social media and not be confronted with the turmoil and hurt in our world. Natural disasters, political haggling, racial strife, famine, war, addictions, pandemics—we lament so much of what's happening in our towns and nation and across the globe. Add to that the personal pain we experience—financial stress, family tensions, physical or mental illness, spiritual battles—and we wonder how and when healing will come.

The prophet Jeremiah lived in a similar time of rampant sin, false worship, and social injustice. The children of Israel had turned away from God and rejected the message the Lord had called Jeremiah to deliver. They even persecuted him for warning of impending disaster. Grieving for what was to come, Jeremiah cried out,

Is there no balm in Gilead?
Is there no physician there?
Why then is there no healing
for the wound of my people?

JEREMIAH 8:22, NIV

Jeremiah's lament refers to the balm of Gilead, a rare salve produced from the resin of trees located in a mountainous region east of the Jordan River. It was known for its salicin-rich content, which acted as a pain reliever. We see this balm first mentioned in Genesis 37:25 as one of several precious commodities the Ishmaelite traders were taking to the land of Egypt when they bought Joseph from his brothers.

Similar ingredients are still used by herbalists today for treating a myriad of ailments: headaches; skin problems such as cuts, wounds, and burns; throat and bronchial conditions; and inflammation and pain from arthritis and rheumatism.

The refrain from a well-known African American spiritual says,

There is a balm in Gilead to make the wounded whole;
There is a balm in Gilead to heal the sin-sick soul.

HEALING BALM

The phrase *balm of Gilead* has come to signify Jesus, the Prince of Peace, "for Christ himself has brought peace to us" (Ephesians 2:14). He is the only cure-all balm that can heal our souls of all their maladies.

If you're burdened by earthly cares, wounds, or ills and your soul is seeking to be soothed and comforted, reach for a generous portion of the balm of Gilead. Jesus paid the ultimate price so you could luxuriate in his peace.

Sit in a quiet place and express your lament about the struggles you're facing. Envision the healing hand of Jesus applying the lovely balm of his peace to your soul. Feel your cares dissipate in the soothing and comforting fragrance of his presence.

Sunrise, Sunset

DAWN IS BREAKING upon another day at Fodderstack Farm, smudging the sky with reds and oranges. As the sun rises over the mountain, morning chores begin: feeding, watering, cleaning.

We who don't live on the farm also have a task that marks the start of the day: We must make a choice. Will we wake up feeling defeated, believing that yesterday's problems or our negative behaviors are irrevocable? That it's impossible to make progress on areas of our souls needing attention? That repetitive failures mean we're horrible people or poor decision-makers? That our challenging circumstances will never improve? Or will we rise with the sun, do the best we can with the day we've been given, and persevere in remaining hopeful that the next twenty-four hours will contain fresh beginnings and better outcomes?

Each day brings the opportunity, from sunrise to sunset, to dust off yesterday's fumbles and foibles and start over. The psalmist says,

The heavens proclaim the glory of God.
The skies display his craftsmanship.

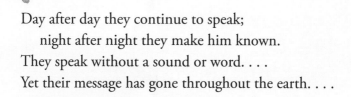

Day after day they continue to speak;
    night after night they make him known.
They speak without a sound or word. . . .
Yet their message has gone throughout the earth. . . .

God has made a home in the heavens for the sun.
It bursts forth like a radiant bridegroom after his wedding.
    It rejoices like a great athlete eager to run the race.
The sun rises at one end of the heavens
    and follows its course to the other end.

PSALM 19:1-6

Isn't it wonderful that the sun continues to rise every morning, signaling a chance to see in it the glory and absolute faithfulness of God? His creativity makes him known to all, securing in our minds the truths that he never changes, that he won't leave us, and that he is the God of second chances. We can start again, radiant in his light.

The psalmist continues with a prayer:

May the words of my mouth
    and the meditation of my heart
be pleasing to you,
    O LORD, my rock and my redeemer.

PSALM 19:14

Each morning, we can come clean before God, shed our crippling guilt, and ask for help to do what pleases him, eager to run the race and change the meditation of our hearts to what delights him. As sure as the sun follows its course, we can rise with hope in the morning and put away our disappointments and despair when the sun sets, looking forward to a new start.

Think about ways you allow your imperfect past to affect your present. Confess them to God, and write a prayer expressing the specific ways you need his help each new day.

Ulysses

ONE FALL DAY, just after Thanksgiving, a lone rooster showed up at Fodderstack Farm. Where he came from was a mystery. What was his story? Did he escape from another farm? Was he lost? Just passing through? The Bakers were leery about his presence, worried he would cause trouble since some roosters are naturally aggressive and will attack humans. Even very gentle breeds can become feisty, and that's why they'd never had a rooster on their farm. They didn't trust him and hoped he was on a journey to somewhere else.

But he stayed on, and they named him Ulysses. It turns out that, surprisingly, he has been a very good rooster. He enthusiastically flaps his wings when he sees a hawk, protecting "his" hens. Ulysses has never exhibited any aggression toward people, and his daily crowing has added to the ambience of the farm. His iridescent feathers shine like jewels in the sun; the beauty of his bright coloring is a delight to the eye.

There's a lesson here for us as humans. How often, when experiencing the presence of someone who is very different from us, do we react with distrust and suspicion? We may jump to stereo-typing people because of the way they look, the color of their skin, the way they dress, their foreign language, or their political views. We allow ourselves to put people into categories based on incorrect information we have gathered about "their kind," perhaps based on our upbringing or a former perception or experience. What rises to the surface is fear rather than the desire to connect. Yet welcoming a stranger is a repeated theme in the Bible, as these passages show:

> Keep on loving each other as brothers and sisters. Don't forget to show hospitality to strangers, for some who have done this have entertained angels without realizing it!
> HEBREWS 13:1-2

> Accept each other just as Christ has accepted you so that God will be given glory.
> ROMANS 15:7

We must remember that everyone has a story. Listening to others talk about their journeys goes a long way to understanding them, which erases our fears about them. How often have we missed the blessing of having a relationship with someone who is not like us, whose beautiful soul could have greatly enriched our lives—all for the glory of God?

Ulysses's appearance on the farm at first caused distrust, suspicion, and fear, but his presence has brought nothing but good things. Even he has a story. We will never know what it is, but it undoubtedly includes being lost, neglected, or mistreated. Because the Bakers gave him a chance to prove he would not be trouble, he has now found a home at Fodderstack Farm and has been embraced as a protector of the other animals. He is in a place where his beauty can be appreciated. And how fun it is to wake each morning to his crowing!

The next time you are inclined to make assumptions about someone before listening to and understanding their story, think about Ulysses. Even a rooster can point to the way of Jesus.

Think about a time when you have resisted connecting with someone different from you. How can you be more welcoming and embracing to the strangers in your life?

Living Bread

WHEN YOU THINK of a farm kitchen, what comes to mind? Perhaps homemade pickles put up in Mason jars, hearty noodle casseroles, fried chicken, cherry pie, or fluffy pancakes with thick-cut bacon. Yet what would a farm kitchen be without homemade bread?

Bread has often been called "the staff of life," an expression that interestingly uses the word *staff* in the sense of a support. It's a very basic food that supports physical life. In the Bible, bread represents spiritual life.

Though the types of bread vary across the world, some form of it is found in virtually every society. For a lot of people, a meal isn't complete unless it includes bread. Is there anything more wonderful than slicing into a warm, crusty, freshly baked loaf? Bread is comfort food, to be sure.

In the first of his "I am" statements, Jesus said, "I am the bread of life. Whoever comes to me will never be hungry again" (John 6:35). Jesus spoke this after he had performed the miracle of turning a young boy's five loaves and two fishes into a meal for five thousand people. The following day, some from the crowd tracked Jesus down and asked him to give them bread every day, just as Moses had given their ancestors manna in the wilderness. Jesus corrected them, telling them it was God who had provided the manna. But because his greater concern was for their spiritual hunger, he also answered by pointing to himself: "The true bread of God is the one who comes down from heaven and gives life to the world" (John 6:33).

People everywhere have an inborn appetite for happiness, peace, and freedom from guilt in their hearts. Unfortunately, they often try to feed that hunger by seeking after wealth, sexual satisfaction, fame, success, power, pleasure, or harmful substances. Many are obsessed with youthfulness and alter their appearance through plastic surgery, and still others are addicted to exercise. Everyone would like to extend their lives as long as possible.

Yet we cannot be truly satisfied by any of these things. Jesus is the only One who can fulfill the hunger of mankind. He said, "Anyone who eats this bread will live forever" (John 6:51). Jesus satisfies the inner yearnings of the human heart by forgiving sins and promising eternal life. He is our real comfort food and the genuine staff of life, our ultimate support.

Are you hungering for something that will satisfy your longings? If you eat from the Bread of Life, you will never be spiritually hungry again. Jesus is the One who came down from heaven to give you a life of purpose, joy, and peace here and now—and eternal life by believing in him.

If you are already a believer, know that God has placed others in your care—your family, your circle of friends, your coworkers—so you can offer them the Bread of Life that they really need. Are you pointing them to this bread by your witness?

In what ways does the Bread of Life provide for your daily spiritual needs? Make a list and write a prayer of gratitude. Ask God to help you share with those in your care the Good News that Jesus can satisfy their every need.

Bread 'n' Butter

What would a farm kitchen be without the aroma of fresh baked goodies wafting through the air, whether a pie cooling on the windowsill, a batch of favorite cookies waiting to be tasted, or a loaf of bread browning in the oven? Baking brings a bit of down-home goodness into your home.

Bread goods that contain yeast in the dough create the best smells, resulting from compounds formed in the fermentation and baking process. Nonyeast treats like muffins and biscuits also smell great once they start to brown, indicating that the heated sugars (present in white sugar, milk or buttermilk, fruit, and even corn) are combining with amino acids, creating not only the appealing golden-brown color but a wonderful tempting aroma as well. Researchers have identified more than twenty compounds that contribute to the aroma of baked goods, the most common scents being milky, buttery, and malty.

Why do we like the smell of bread? One reason is that bread was often a large part of our childhood diets, so its aroma evokes strong memories of family and comfort. A 2017 Irish study found that 89 percent of people said the smell of bread made them happy, and a French study found the aroma of freshly baked bread can not only put you in a better mood but also make you kinder toward others.

Not a baker? Get up early, find a bakery, and pick up a loaf or two. If you're not an early riser, consider buying frozen dough available at the supermarket. There are many ways to enjoy bread—toasted, grilled, oven-warmed, or cold. Build a sandwich, use it as a base for cheese and/or vegetable toppings, or simply spread on some tasty butter.

Butter? Yum! Take it to the next level by creating custom flavors with tasty add-ins, creating what's known by foodies as "compound butter." Many meats and savory dishes can be enhanced by compound butters made with garlic, herbs, and other robust seasonings, while baked breads and treats are taken to the next level with honey, cinnamon, maple syrup, nuts, or fruit.

Just about anything that would pair well with bread, toast, croissants, rolls, biscuits, muffins, pancakes, and waffles can be blended into butter for ready-to-serve deliciousness. Start by ensuring that a stick of quality butter is at room temperature; then place it in a bowl and mix in your finely chopped ingredients for whatever flavor profile you want to try. Place the mixture on wax paper and roll it into a log shape. To store, wrap the paper around the log and twist the ends. Flavored butter will last in your refrigerator up to a few weeks, or longer in the freezer. There's nothing like the taste and smell of a warm baked treat with flavorful butter to bring a touch of farm-kitchen comfort to your table.

Yummy Compound Butter Flavors to Try with Baked Goods

- Cinnamon Honey
- Cinnamon Brown Sugar
- Honey Walnut (or Pecan)
- Blueberry Lavender
- Garlic Parmesan
- Tomato and Basil
- Strawberry
- Gingerbread
- Pecan Praline
- Cranberry and Walnut
- Chocolate — what's not to love?
- Orange Maple
- Cherry Sage
- Pumpkin Spice
- Coffee and Cream

Eunice and Little Blackie

WHEN THE OWNERS of a farm in Tennessee had gotten too old to care for their sheep, the Bakers adopted five of them—the first to live at Fodderstack Farm. Drew and Renee learned that each one had a unique personality, temperament, and taste in friends. Eunice, whose name comes from the word *ewe* (a female sheep), was an older Katahdin/Suffolk mix. Because she had been bottle-fed by her shepherd, she was the friendliest of the group and would often approach her new owners asking for love and attention.

After a few years, the Bakers noticed that Eunice would stand in the middle of the pasture all alone, bleating to her flock, even during the night. The farm veterinarian, Dr. Vicky, determined that Eunice had lost her sight. She suggested that Drew and Renee try to identify her best sheep friend so they could place a belled collar around his neck. After watching closely, they determined it was Little Blackie. Amazingly, the sound of Little Blackie's bell allowed Eunice to follow him around and stay safely within the flock for the rest of her life.

Friendship is one of God's greatest gifts. We are all in need of people who can provide a safe haven in our lives. It's a great pleasure to share companionship and camaraderie in the good times, when we can laugh and have fun together. But the best friendships may be those that provide the guidance, care, and support we desperately need when we've lost our way or become blind to the truth—when in our darkness we are led like Eunice and kept safely in the fold, through thick and thin, in the storms and in the sun. And we have the blessing of doing the same for them.

Perhaps you've already experienced a time when you were lost, walking around in the darkness of spiritual blindness, and someone led you with the bell of God's truth into the Good Shepherd's fold. Or maybe you've had the privilege of guiding a friend who has no spiritual sight. Ecclesiastes 4:9-10 sums it up well: "Two people are better off than one, for they can help each other succeed. If one person falls, the other can reach out and help. But someone who falls alone is in real trouble."

Think of some of the ways your friends have been there when you've needed them most. Thank God for each one, and write them a note of appreciation. Next, think of someone who lacks spiritual eyes for seeing life the way that God does; commit to being God's bell-wearer for that person as you reach out in friendship.

Bambi

IT'S A STANDARD Fodderstack Farm routine to count noses, making sure all the animals are accounted for. One day in late fall, Drew came up one sheep short, which is unusual since sheep usually stay together. After surveying the flock, he realized that Bambi was missing.

All the pasture gates were open so the sheep could wander to the best grass, enlarging the search area. Bambi wasn't in the donkey shed, the sheep sheds, or the horse barn, so Drew searched the entire west field, looking behind the hills and large trees. Still no Bambi.

Then Drew thought of the multiflora rose bushes in the far corner of the main pasture—nasty plants with long, tentacle-like vines and sharp thorns. The Bakers had tried to eliminate the nuisances, but they're tough to kill. Drew knew of a few still growing on a nearby ridge.

Sure enough, when Drew came to the crest of the hill, he found Bambi completely ensnared. While trying to escape, he had twisted and turned until the thorny plant roped itself around his body and legs. Like most herd animals, sheep don't call out when they're in trouble because they're afraid of attracting predators—so it's up to the shepherd to find them.

Wearing his deerskin gloves, Drew was able to arduously untangle the hurting sheep. Bambi didn't struggle against the efforts but patiently lay there as Drew worked for forty minutes to extricate him. When Bambi was free, Drew picked him up, brought him back to the main pasture, and offered him food and water.

Both Drew and Renee watched as Bambi tried to walk away, badly cut and limping from the thorns. They decided to call Dr. Vicky. She backed her truck right up to the barn when she arrived and proceeded to x-ray Bambi's leg. The poor creature had a slight fracture from his struggle to escape, so Dr. Vicky applied salve to his wounds, gave him a shot of antibiotics, and splinted his leg, taping and wrapping it in a waterproof cover.

Bambi hobbled off to his flock, all of whom sniffed him to make sure he was okay. The splint stayed on for four weeks, and he limped for a few weeks afterward. But the Bakers are happy to report that now he's as good as new.

Just as Drew looked for Bambi, our Good Shepherd cares enough to seek us out when we are lost. Then he binds our wounds and heals us. How wonderful to think that heaven rejoices when one lost sinner repents and returns to God!

If a man has a hundred sheep and one of them gets lost,
what will he do? Won't he leave the ninety-nine others in the
wilderness and go to search for the one that is lost until he
finds it? And when he has found it, he will joyfully carry it

home on his shoulders. When he arrives, he will call together
his friends and neighbors, saying, "Rejoice with me because
I have found my lost sheep." In the same way, there is more
joy in heaven over one lost sinner who repents and returns
to God than over ninety-nine others who are righteous and
haven't strayed away!

LUKE 15:4-7

How has God sought you out when you have strayed? Journal
your gratitude to your Good Shepherd.

Shearing Day

IT'S SHEEP-SHEARING DAY AT Fodderstack Farm. Each spring, the traveling shearer, who looks like everyone's vision of a mountain man, goes from farm to farm performing this important service.

Fiber sheep don't shed, so they must be shorn to maintain their health and hygiene. Ewes are shorn before lambing, making it easier for their newborns to nurse in a cleaner environment. Excess wool can cause skin to become irritated and infected when dirt, manure, and scraps of food become trapped, attracting flies and other pests. Large amounts of wool can also immobilize sheep, making them susceptible to attacks by predators and likely to fall backward when they're on an incline due to the weight of their coats. "Wool blindness" can also result when long wool covers their eyes. Worst of all, the sheep may become overheated, which can lead to death.

It's fascinating to watch the shearing. The apprehensive sheep are put into a holding pen, then let out individually and caught by the shearer, who gently places them on their backs. They become docile, and the shearer takes them in hand, knowing exactly how to handle them. In a quick and efficient set of movements, the wool is shorn in large sections without cutting the skin, taking about three to four minutes. It is then gathered and sorted for the softest wool, then scoured, picked apart, and collected into fibers. Sheep don't like shearing day, but they enjoy being relieved of their heavy wool coats.

In its just-shorn state, the wool is not clean, white, and fluffy as we may imagine; it's dark, dirty, and unattractive. Only after being thoroughly skirted (pulling off the undesirable parts) and washed does it resemble what we think of as wool ready for the spinning wheel. Shearing day is the beginning of a process that ends with beautiful skeins of yarn that Renee has spun and colored with natural dyes from the cutting garden. She then crafts the yarn into one-of-a-kind knitted pieces.

Once again, in the life of animals we find wonderful illustrations of important lessons for people. It's vital for *our* spiritual health to allow our heavenly Shearer to cut back harmful things of this world that "stick" to us. Otherwise we may begin to "lose our cool" by allowing anger to turn to bitterness. When we let unconfessed sins remain embedded in our hearts, they can fester and infect us and lead to more sin. Then we may fall and become less capable of fleeing the attacks of the predator of our souls, losing sight of God's best for us.

Isaiah 1:18 says, "Though [your sins] are red like crimson, I will make them as white as wool." We need our heavenly Shearer to regularly care for our spiritual well-being. He knows exactly how to handle us. What a relief to let him remove what's not pleasing to him and others, lighten our loads, take our sins, restore our vision, and turn us into people who are clean and useful in beautiful ways.

Meditate on Hebrews 12:1: "Let us strip off every weight that slows us down, especially the sin that so easily trips us up." Then journal your thoughts on how you may need God's tending.

The Shepherd's Psalm

WE CANNOT VISIT Fodderstack Farm—a sheep farm where the Bakers devotedly watch over their flock—without considering the beloved Twenty-Third Psalm. David, the author of this psalm and the king of Israel, was a former shepherd, and his language in this metaphor shows he knew intimately how to convey God's character and his relationship to his children.

Charles Spurgeon wrote, "David himself had been a keeper of the sheep and understood both the needs of the sheep and the many cares of a shepherd. He compares himself to a creature weak, defenseless, and foolish, and he takes God to be his Provider, Preserver, Director and, indeed, his everything."

The psalm's comforting words paint a beautiful picture of a loving Father's goodness to his children in every life circumstance.

Verse 1: *The LORD is my shepherd; I have all that I need.*
There is no "I hope" or "maybe" but only "The Lord *is* my shepherd" (present tense). He is *my* shepherd, and we

know each other intimately. He cares for every one of *my* needs; I want for nothing, present or future. I can lean into our relationship with total confidence and rely on him journeying with me.

Verse 2: *He lets me rest in green meadows; he leads me beside peaceful streams.* He knows I need rest (physical blessing) and calmness (spiritual blessing). The pastures where he takes me are lush, and the waters are still and relaxing.

Verse 3: *He renews my strength. He guides me along right paths, bringing honor to his name.* The only one who can do this restorative, healing work in my soul is God. He leads me in the best path for my life and teaches me to live righteously. He has given me a high purpose—to glorify him.

Verse 4: *Even when I walk through the darkest valley, I will not be afraid, for you are close beside me. Your rod and your staff protect and comfort me.* In foreboding times, when I am surrounded by darkness and overwhelmed by the evil in the world, I need not fear. When death threatens, our faithful God is always nearby. I am corrected by his rod when I go astray and protected and comforted by the staff of his presence.

Verse 5: *You prepare a feast for me in the presence of my enemies. You honor me by anointing my head with oil. My cup overflows with blessings.* Even when I face enemies of all kinds, he puts me in a place of honor right in front of them, where I feast abundantly at his table and am given everything I need to be victorious. This gives me great hope.

Verse 6: *Surely your goodness and unfailing love will pursue me all the days of my life, and I will live in the house of the LORD forever.* He has ordained all my days. I can count on his presence following me and am blessed with his kindness. His love never fails. My eternal future is secure.

Reread these reflections on Psalm 23 and journal the experiences that affirm how God provides for you as the Good Shepherd.

Keeping Sheep

Few scenes are as cute as fluffy lambs frolicking through a field or as idyllic as sheep grazing on a green hillside. An iconic part of farm life, sheep have been raised since ancient times for both their meat and wool.

Sheep are one of the earliest domesticated animals known. Originally kept by nomadic peoples in ancient Mesopotamia, sheep gradually scattered across the earth as people groups migrated and explorers came to the New World. The first domestic sheep arrived in North America with Christopher Columbus. Colonists and settlers found sheep invaluable, and flocks eventually spread throughout Mexico and the southwestern US.

Most sheep in America are owned by large producers located primarily in western states, where large flocks graze on the open range. Small flocks are increasing, however, especially in the eastern half of the country and on farms that favor sustainable practices.

Sheep are fairly defenseless against predators, naturally nervous, and easily frightened. Farmers often use guardian dogs to help protect their flocks. A trained herding dog is also helpful for managing sheep; they work in partnership with their handlers, obeying commands and using calm authority to coax the sheep to move where the shepherd directs.

And now to the cute stuff—lambs. Typically born in the spring, often in litters of one to three and with an average weight of eight to ten pounds, lambs are like other baby animals—they sleep a lot (eight to twelve hours a day), are very curious, and like to play. Lambs tend to stay close to their mom until they are weaned at about two months old. After that, they spend most of their time in the pasture grazing, exploring, and romping about with their friends.

At least once a year, sheep need a haircut so they don't become uncomfortable and stressed; it also prevents their wool from becoming matted and hard to shear. Shearing doesn't hurt the sheep, yet it does require skill. The fleece is removed in one piece—usually with electric shears or a shearing machine, but it can also be done by hand. Many farmers hire professionals who can shear a sheep in less than two minutes.

Wool is a great insulator, making it ideal for making blankets, sweaters, socks, scarves, and hats. It is also ideal for camping and outdoor use since it absorbs water, keeping skin dry, warm, and comfortable. Wool is also extremely durable and holds up well to wear and tear, making it an ideal material for rugs.

Sheep are not easy animals to keep unless you have time, space, and access to grazing pastures. But everyone can appreciate their beauty and seek opportunities to support small sheep farmers, purchase products made of local wool, or visit a children's zoo during lambing or shearing season.

Sheep as Pets

Sheep make good pets because they are gentle and respond well to human contact. Bottle-feeding a lamb works well because it creates a bond of trust. Pet sheep should be females or neutered males, and it's best if they are "hair" breeds—with a coat like other animals—since they won't require shearing, as "wool" breeds do. Sheep are social animals, so having at least two, or preferably a small flock of five to six, is most desirable.

Sheep: Did You Know?

Various parts of sheep are used to make items such as yarn, insulation, tennis balls, baseballs, upholstery, chewing gum, industrial oils, cosmetics, ceramics, medicines, crayons, candles, creams and lotions, surgical sutures, piano keys, adhesive tape, buttons, ice cream, shampoo and conditioner, crochet needles, and much more!

Children on the Farm

CHILDREN HAVE BEEN among the most delighted of the Bakers' guests at Fodderstack Farm—some of whom had never before been on a farm or had only seen animals at the zoo. They hadn't encountered the opportunity to interact with animals closely. In the guest book we find expressions of this joy:

> "Who knew that a group of chickens could be so full of riotous entertainment for all three generations of our family. Our daughter Ella discovered the beauty of poaching the freshest eggs ever."

> "Drew and Renee taught us all so much about the different animals and encouraged the children to help with feeding, grooming, and caring for them. They learned to be respectful of the animals and to get to know them."

Discovering the simple pleasures of farm life can be superbly enriching for children whose lives are often filled with technology, screens, competitive sports, and other complexities of life. How wonderful that these parents wanted to pass down a love for animals to their children and thought it important they have these experiences. The Bakers show these kids not only the rules on how animals are to be treated, but also the wonders of their beauty, characteristics, and personalities.

But how much more important it is for Christian parents to pass on to their children the treasures of the Bible. The Word tells us,

> You must commit yourselves wholeheartedly to these
> commands that I am giving you today. Repeat them again
> and again to your children. Talk about them when you are at
> home and when you are on the road, when you are going to
> bed and when you are getting up.

DEUTERONOMY 6:6-7

> We will tell the next generation
> about the glorious deeds of the LORD,
>   about his power and his mighty wonders. . . .
> He commanded our ancestors
>   to teach them to their children,
> so the next generation might know them. . . .
> So each generation should set its hope anew on God,
>   not forgetting his glorious miracles
>   and obeying his commands.

PSALM 78:4-7

Clearly we are not only to pass on the commands and truths of the Lord to children, but also *how* to know him—to tell of his wonders, miracles, and glorious deeds so they can set their hopes on him. If you are a parent or someone who has nurturing relationships with young nieces, nephews, cousins, or friends' children, you are charged with finding creative ways to fulfill this important task.

For example, you can give them opportunities to enjoy nature and celebrate its beauty; share stories of how God has been at work in the lives of your ancestors and your own life; or take them to Sunday School—perhaps even serving as a teacher. And be encouraged knowing that your investment will bring a large return. Proverbs 22:6 says, "Direct your children onto the right path, and when they are older, they will not leave it."

How can you best build into the children in your life and pass on the hope of the Lord?

Canine Sunbathers

THE BAKERS' ADORABLE DOGS—Darla, a Japanese Chin rescue, and Tucker, a mixed-breed rescue—are two very beloved animals at Fodderstack Farm.

On any given day they may be found sprawled out on the rug, basking in the large patch of sunlight coming in from the farm-house's French doors. They occasionally shift their positions between snoozes, completely content to just lie there soaking in the warmth. Eventually they relocate from room to room, looking for the current bright spots on the floor as the sun moves across the sky. They love the sunlight. They are light-seekers.

The Bible has much to say about light. Here are a few examples:

Jesus . . . said, "I am the light of the world. If you follow me,
you won't have to walk in darkness, because you will have
the light that leads to life."

JOHN 8:12

At one time you were darkness, but now you are light in the Lord. Walk as children of light.

EPHESIANS 5:8, ESV

There's something so beautiful about the image of these sun-bathing dogs, deliberately lounging in and following the light, drinking in its warmth—a metaphor for who we are and what we must do as believers. We who follow the One who called himself the light of the world are referred to in the same way. We are called to be light bearers. Jesus said, "You are the light of the world—like a city on a hilltop that cannot be hidden. No one lights a lamp and then puts it under a basket. Instead, a lamp is placed on a stand, where it gives light to everyone in the house" (Matthew 5:14-15).

To serve as light bearers, we must first be filled with the light ourselves. We bask in God's presence when we spend time in silence, prayer, and the Bible. When we have been with Jesus, it will show; God bathes us in his light, and it cannot be concealed. He uses us to radiate its warmth into the cold world around us. As we project the fruit of the Spirit—love, joy, peace, patience, kindness, goodness, faithfulness, gentleness, and self-control—people are attracted to our light. We can do this by accepting them when no one else does, going the extra mile to help them, offering words of encouragement, or just being a good listener.

To quote Madeleine L'Engle, "We draw people to Christ not . . . by telling them how wrong they are and how right we are, but by showing them a light that is so lovely that they want with all their hearts to know the source of it." Can others see that you are a follower of the Light of the World by your words and deeds?

Make a list of specific ways you can reflect his light to those around you—coworkers, neighbors, family, friends, or the cashier at the grocery store. Then meditate on this verse: "God, who said, 'Let there be light in the darkness,' has made this light shine in our hearts so we could know the glory of God that is seen in the face of Jesus Christ" (2 Corinthians 4:6).

Summit Climbing

THE BLUE RIDGE MOUNTAINS surrounding Fodderstack Farm are named for the bluish haze that frequently encompasses them. They provide many opportunities for climbing types, beckoning adventure seekers to lace up their hiking boots.

One peak, Mount Pisgah, rises sharply from Pisgah National Forest and offers stunning views from its mountaintop observation deck. The trail meanders with many switchbacks through a lush deciduous forest filled with wildflowers, vibrant green moss, tall grasses, leafy ferns, and lichen-crusted rocks. While it's a gentle climb at first, the second half is an unrelenting reach to the top, passing over rustic stone stairs and challenging rocky outcrops as it gains elevation. Then it dives through a thick ceiling of mountain laurel branches that twist and turn overhead. Abundant light suddenly fills the trail as the hike ascends through the dense forest canopy to the sun-drenched peak. The summit offers spectacular views in every direction.

Like a long mountain climb, we're at the trailhead of our journey of sanctification when we newly come to the Lord. We can see the summit and glimpse the climb, which doesn't seem difficult. With excitement and enthusiasm, we may think the way will be smooth and trouble-free.

But the trek is never a straight shot to perfection. Our path to holiness meanders and veers off in different directions. There are manageable stretches and beautiful sights all along the climb but also challenging pathways blocked by difficulties that seem like huge rocks to scale, testing our perseverance. We lose sight of the summit sometimes and wonder whether we'll ever get there. It can get stormy; the path can be obscured, and we may lose our way. We stumble and become weary; our legs burn with fatigue, and we begin to doubt whether we can take another step.

But when we pray for strength and guidance, God graciously renews us with his power to keep going and points the way with his infinite wisdom. And the reward? We grow in faith and become stronger in the process, increasingly learning to rely on God, trusting him to take our hand and guide us ever upward. For it's the journey that forms and transforms us.

By keeping our eyes on the sunny summit—our heavenly home where we will finally be perfect—we will reach our destination and see things clearly instead of as "puzzling reflections in a mirror" (1 Corinthians 13:12). And it's then we can say, "I have fought the good fight, I have finished the race, and I have remained faithful" (2 Timothy 4:7).

The view will be spectacular!

Meditate on the promises in the following verses. Then write down some ways God has already kept them in your life, and thank him for his faithfulness to you.

"God is my strong fortress, and he makes my way perfect. He makes me as surefooted as a deer, enabling me to stand on mountain heights" (2 Samuel 22:33-34).

"Come, let us go up to the mountain of the LORD.... There he will teach us his ways, and we will walk in his paths" (Isaiah 2:3).

Refining Fire

WE'VE ALL HEARD the warning, "If you play with fire, you're going to get burned." As children we're taught to stay away from the stove and fireplace, and as adults our images of hell are informed by the Bible's description of a "fiery lake" (Revelation 20:10) where "the fire never goes out" (Mark 9:48).

The word *fire* can bring unpleasant earthly images to mind as well. Carelessly lit forest fires are often hard to contain and devastate acres of vegetation, animal habitats, family homes, and vital businesses, and fires set off by neglected space heaters and faulty appliances also have the potential for causing heartbreaking destruction.

But fire can also be a valuable tool. Farmers use "controlled fires," or "prescribed burns," to reveal mineral layers in the soil that will increase seedling vitality. Forest managers use them to stimulate the germination of desirable trees; there are scheduled controlled burns in the Pisgah National Forest for this reason. Gardeners use them with a classification of plants known as "fire followers," such as the fire poppy, since burnt soil signals them to sprout and bloom. Prairie conservationists also use them for hazard reduction, decreasing the likelihood that more serious fires will occur.

There are times in life when it seems like we, too, are enduring a hot fire: the burn of a relationship gone bad or the conflagration of a failed business deal, the sting of chronic physical or emotional pain, the sear of unrelenting grief or scorching temptation. Our feet are held to the flames of circumstances that threaten to consume us.

But just as farmers, foresters, gardeners, and prairie conservationists use controlled burns, God is using these experiences in our lives to bring increased vitality to the seeds of our faith and a beneficial growth of virtues in our character. He uses them to eliminate elements in our lives that could potentially cause more serious fires. And sometimes it's only in the burnt soil that we can bloom as beautifully as he intended.

God is very intentional in how he allows the fire to accomplish this purpose in our lives. Let the following Scriptures encourage you as you meditate on the ways he has used these times of refinement for the building up of your faith:

When you walk through fire you shall not be burned,
    and the flame shall not consume you.

ISAIAH 43:2, ESV

These trials will show that your faith is genuine. It is being tested as fire tests and purifies gold—though your faith is far more precious than mere gold. So when your faith remains strong through many trials, it will bring you much praise and glory and honor on the day when Jesus Christ is revealed to the whole world.

1 PETER 1:7

After you have suffered a little while, he will restore, support, and strengthen you, and he will place you on a firm foundation.

1 PETER 5:10

Looking back, can you describe how God has used fiery trials in your life to bring about positive results in your walk of faith? Write a prayer asking God to help you trust him in the hard times.

Beekeeping

Heard the buzz? Bees. Bees. Bees. It's estimated that up to 125,000 people in the US now keep bees, both as a hobby and commercially. Good for the environment and beneficial for your yard and garden, bees mostly take care of themselves—and the result is homegrown honey to sweeten your table or to sell for income.

Bees are also fascinating creatures, and the life of the colony is filled with both the dramatic and the miraculous. Each colony has one queen bee, the only egg layer, and is usually supported by tens of thousands of worker bees (underdeveloped females) and hundreds of males (whose only job is to mate with a new queen).

Before you "buzz" out to get bees, get prepared. Do some research, find a local mentor or beekeeping group, and check with your local authorities for guidelines or restrictions. Find a corner of your property where you can create an apiary—a collection of wooden hive boxes where the bees will live and build their honeycombs. Place it close enough to your house so it's convenient to check on the hives, and be sure to protect it from extreme sun and wind.

Bees, like all creatures, need water, so if you don't have a natural water source, simply set up a birdbath and add some rocks so they have a place to land. They also need a food source, and although they will forage up to several miles away, you may want to plant bee-friendly herbs, flowers, and vegetables nearby.

Like any hobby, beekeeping requires supplies. No matter your budget level, the important thing is that you are prepared and protected. A beekeeper's "veil" is essential—a hat with a screen for your head and face. A beekeeper's suit is nice to have as well, but a heavy jacket, long pants, and gloves will suffice, but be sure to close off the openings at the ankles and wrists to prevent the bees from getting in your clothing (duct tape works great).

You'll also want a bee smoker, which helps calm the bees when you're working with the hives; a small pry bar or tool to help loosen the hive tops and frames; and a firm brush to brush the bees off the frames. After a few seasons are under your belt, you might want to invest in a honey extractor, which helps in removing the honey from the hives.

A successful beekeeper will nurture the colony so it has the most bees precisely when the local nectar flows, allowing for maximum honey production. The beekeeper will also breed a new queen, allowing the start of a new colony; and to keep the colony together, he or she will work to control the bees' swarming impulse.

Beekeeping is a rewarding hobby, and it's good for the planet. It takes years of learning and experience to successfully manage all aspects of beekeeping, but beginners can still achieve a good honey harvest. A productive colony will make more honey than its bees need—and the surplus is yours to enjoy!

Beekeeping: Did You Know?

- Ancient Egyptians practiced beekeeping using hives made by mixing straw and clay.

- Artificial hives with varying designs have been used over the centuries. Today's most common structure originates from Lorenzo Langstroth, a Massachusetts school principal who patented his design in 1852.

- The easiest way to start your colony is to buy bees from a local beekeeping organization. Consult the website for the American Beekeeping Federation for a list of active groups in your area (abfnet.org/page/states).

Darkness and Light

ONE FEBRUARY NIGHT at Fodderstack Farm, the eerie sound of coyotes on the prowl filled the chilly air. Their plaintive howls came close to the farmhouse as they searched for food. The big concern was for the young sheep, who would be easy prey under the cover of darkness.

Because coyotes avoid people and light, Dr. Vicky, the farm vet, recommended that the young ones be kept in the paddock nearest the house, with battery-powered candles placed around its perimeter. Meanwhile, the donkeys patrolled the pasture. Thankfully the strategy worked! The coyotes were deterred by both the flickering light of the candles that pierced the darkness and the proximity of the people and house. Kept away from the darkness and isolation, the young lambs were safe.

Like nocturnal predators, those intent on doing harm often wait until nighttime to carry out their plans, using the darkness to increase their chances of not being discovered. John 3:19-21 tells us, "God's light came into the world, but people loved the darkness more than the light, for their actions were evil. All who do evil hate the light and refuse to go near it for fear their sins will be exposed. But those who do what is right come to the light so others can see that they are doing what God wants."

The light has come. Jesus said, "I am the light of the world. If you follow me, you won't have to walk in darkness, because you will have the light that leads to life" (John 8:12).

Unbelievers remain in the dark, where sins cannot be seen and death prevails. But when someone decides to follow Christ, his or her sins are exposed by the light, where they can be repented of and forgiven. In the light there is life.

Sometimes even believers are living in rebellion against God in an area of their lives. It's natural to want to keep our wrongdoing shrouded in the dark and hidden from God, even though we know he sees and knows all. We try to hide from others as well for fear they may find us out.

But when we come into the light of God's offer of mercy and grace, he shines his unconditional love on us, and we have the wonderful privilege of confessing our sin and receiving his forgiveness. James 5:16 says, "Confess your sins to each other and pray for each other so that you may be healed." Oh, the great relief of walking completely in the light!

Is there something in your life you're keeping in the darkness? Maybe you're carrying guilt and shame for something in your past, a matter you've shared with no one. Or perhaps there's something in the present—a behavior, a way of thinking, a grudge you are holding—that's keeping you from living in the freedom that comes from a clean heart. Confess everything by writing out an earnest prayer below. Then focus on receiving God's forgiveness by faith and expressing your thanksgiving to him in return.

Craft Therapy

FODDERSTACK FARM is a place where a lot of crafting takes place, such as soapmaking and lotion making. Renee's favorite activity is spinning the sheep's wool into yarn, then using natural dyes from the flowers and plants she grows in her cutting garden to make beautifully colored skeins. She knits the yarn into scarves, shawls, sweaters, throws, and the like—all reflecting the farm's animals and plants.

At a time when the digital world is overwhelming, people are turning to crafts as an antidote to the stressful feelings that arise from modern living. In his book *Flow: The Psychology of Optimal Experience*, psychologist Mihaly Csikszentmihalyi explains how crafting allows us to enter into a "flow" state—a perfect immersive state of balance between skill and challenge. Mindfulness.

Taking a cue from how occupational therapists used activities such as basket weaving and knitting to help veterans of World Wars I and II recover from shell shock, crafts are now used to treat post-traumatic stress disorder (PTSD), depression, chronic fatigue syndrome, and anorexia. Researchers continue to seek understanding of how craft activities benefit body and mind. God, as ultimate Creator, made people in his image and placed a creative impulse into each of us. Of the woman in Proverbs 31, we learn,

> She finds wool and flax
> and busily spins it. . . .
> She plants a vineyard. . . .
> Her hands are busy spinning thread,
> her fingers twisting fiber. . . .
> She makes her own bedspreads. . . .
> She makes belted linen garments
> and sashes to sell to the merchants.
>
> PROVERBS 31:13, 16, 19, 22, 24

The Bible speaks of both men and women who engaged in many types of crafts: jewelers, engravers, goldsmiths and silversmiths, gardeners, bakers, blacksmiths, wood-carvers, stone setters, makers of textiles, spinners, vintners, cloth and wool dyers, embroiderers, tentmakers, perfumers, and soapmakers.

In Exodus 31:1-11 and Exodus 36:1-7, we learn how God used craftsmen in the construction of the Temple, including Bezalel from the tribe of Judah, whom he "filled . . . with the Spirit of God" (31:3). He also appointed Oholiab as Bezalel's assistant. Exodus 35:35 tells us the Lord gave them "special skills as engravers, designers, embroiderers in blue, purple, and scarlet thread on fine linen cloth, and weavers." Notice that it was *the Spirit of God* who gave

Bezalel the crafting skill, ability, and knowledge to make the artistic designs. He was in "the flow state" of the Holy Spirit.

For many of us today, this God-given creativity remains hidden and unused. But using our hands artistically can be very therapeutic, and with some trial and error, time and dedication, we might find a craft in which we can actually experience success. Then we can discover the benefits of the mindful "flow state," finding enjoyment and balance in our otherwise stressful lives.

Is there a craft in which you've had an interest but have never tried? Jot down anything that you'd like to explore and do a little research on what you need to start; then record it here.

Hoof Trimming

THE PASTURE ANIMALS at Fodderstack Farm have hooves that are growing all the time and must be watched carefully; if left unchecked, overgrown hooves become misshapen and uncomfortable. The animals begin to limp in pain and may even end up on their knees, nearly immobile—easy prey for predators and unable to eat to survive. For the young, this can quickly turn tragic.

Rooster Cogburn has no horseshoes, so it's important that his hooves are trimmed by his skilled and caring farrier, Jessica, every six weeks. The donkeys get theirs trimmed every three months, and the sheep once a year when sheared. Trimming hooves requires a very sharp tool, and some animals are less cooperative than others, thinking the procedure is punishment. The donkeys may kick and fight, so the Bakers either give them a sedative or hold them still until they calm down and learn they can't kick their way out of a trimming.

Can you see the parallel to the Christian life? Hebrews 12:6 says, "The LORD disciplines those he loves." We, too, require "trimming" in our walk with the Lord so we can overcome the sin that besets us, growing in spiritual health. Like the pasture animals on the farm, we don't get very excited about the prospect of God taking a sharp tool to us. Discipline is not a pleasurable experience.

But if we kick and fight and try to avoid it, we may bring even more pain and trouble into our lives, leaving us unable to do the work God has designed us for. We may not love it, but we can be more open to learning from his correction, lest we begin to limp and struggle or even end up on our knees.

Proverbs 12:1 says, "To learn, you must love discipline; it is stupid to hate correction." If we try to avoid the sometimes painful discipline of our Father, we may think we're getting away with something, but we are really only hurting ourselves. Clearly there is wisdom in accepting the times when God needs to rein us in. In the long run, we will reap the benefits of it. The words of Hebrews 12:11 tell us, "No discipline is enjoyable while it is happening—it's painful! But afterward there will be a peaceful harvest of right living for those who are trained in this way."

God loves and cares for us and understands exactly how to train us. Just as the Bakers, as good shepherds, know how to best care for their animals, we need to have what's harmful trimmed away from our lives, letting our Good Shepherd shape our souls in such a way that we can live righteously and in peace.

Job 5:17 reminds us, "Consider the joy of those corrected by God! Do not despise the discipline of the Almighty when you sin." We may not feel happy and joyful when disciplined, but we can have an open heart to accept it more willingly.

Write a prayer thanking your Good Shepherd for loving you enough to correct you and asking him to make you more open to his discipline.

Fallow Times

FARMERS USE FALLOW PERIODS to maintain the natural productivity of their land, allowing an area that is normally planted to be left inactive for a season so it can recover its fertility. On Fodderstack Farm, this means the animals eat the grass in three pastures according to a specific plan. Each pasture is then able to rebalance its soil nutrients so it can stay healthy and continue to provide bountiful food for the animals.

People, too, need fallow seasons in their lives—times to rest, replenish, and reset. Some of us don't know how to do this, or at least we find it very hard. We're so used to being busy that we find it unsettling when life's momentum stops, either because of a circumstance, such as an illness or the loss of a job, or by choice—when we realize that we *need* to slow down. Even then we become anxious and want to return to our fast-paced routines.

But these down times can be a blessing that frees us to be quiet and listen to what God is saying, bringing clarity to our priorities and reorienting us to his plan. Like the pasture grass lying fallow, the purpose is to recover so we can flourish for the long run. Our souls should be allowed to rest, to be renourished by stretches of peaceful, undisturbed time.

Not everyone's circumstances allow the luxury of taking long periods of rest, but you can build in certain times during the week for renewal. God created the Sabbath for just this purpose. Hebrews 4:9-10 says, "There is a special rest still waiting for the people of God. For all who have entered into God's rest have rested from their labors, just as God did after creating the world."

We may feel selfish for taking time out, or we may tell ourselves we can't afford to take a break; but the truth is that we require these periods in our lives. Burning out hurts us emotionally, mentally, physically, and spiritually. We need to pay attention to the signs that indicate it's time to lie fallow. If we ignore them, the pressure will only intensify until we have no choice but to take time off.

So at a minimum, taking a cue from our Creator, it's possible to set aside the seventh day for rest. Eventually we can add on to this intentional practice by taking a vacation or setting aside a day or two to just do nothing. It may not be for an entire season, as with the pastures on the farm, but with some creativity, we can reorder our lives to include these needed fallow times.

List and think about some specific ways you can make
necessary changes to your schedule so they include times
of restoration and renewal for your soul.

Home Canning

Whether you've planted your garden in a spacious backyard plot or in a few containers on your deck, your green thumb has proven successful, and now your kitchen is overflowing with produce. Don't know what to do with it all? Try home canning!

Not just something Grandma used to do, canning can be a fun and economical way to make fresh foods available year-round. Time spent preserving your spring and summer bounty will stock your pantry with healthy and delicious fruits and vegetables.

Home canning uses heat to destroy organisms that cause fruits and veggies to spoil, then preserves the produce for months or years in vacuum-sealed glass jars. Preserving fresh food with salt, sugar, and vinegar (pickling) has been around for centuries, but it wasn't until the early 1800s that the modern canning process was invented by the French for preserving meat, fruit, vegetables, and even milk to feed their armies. In the United States, home canning peaked in World War II when citizens were encouraged to garden as a way of supporting the war effort.

Safe home-canning methods include boiling-water-bath canning and pressure canning. The method used depends on the foods you want to preserve. The boiling-water-bath method is easy and safe, and there's no need to buy an expensive canner. Ideal for high-acid foods such as citrus fruits, berries, peaches, pickles, and pickled vegetables, foods preserved by the water-bath method are as rich in dietary fiber and vitamins as their fresh or frozen counterparts (and sometimes more so).

Meats and low-acid vegetables must be processed in a pressure canner, the only processing method that reaches the high temperature needed to safely preserve these foods. Good for stews, soups, spaghetti, and almost all vegetables, pressure canning requires a heavy-duty cooker with a steam-tight cover and a pressure gauge. A pressure canner can usually be purchased at a home-goods store or online.

After familiarizing yourself with the process and equipment, start by preparing the food you'll be canning. Then simply load the jars, tighten the rims and lids, and set the jars into your canner. Follow the directions for processing your specific food at the proper pressure and the required length of time; then release the pressure and cool the jars to complete the sealing process.

If you are ready to turn your bounty into a blessing, purchase a good book about home canning, or find a reliable internet source for current information. Then savor discovering the joy of this tried-and-true farm tradition!

Home Canning Tips:

- Can your fruits and vegetables immediately after harvest.

- Choose only fresh, firm produce.

- Wash produce thoroughly.

- Never use a lid that is not a home-canning lid.

- Never reuse lids for canning; it is a common (and dangerous) cause of a failed seal.

Starry, Starry Night

MANY VISITORS to Fodderstack Farm are urban dwellers looking to escape the hustle and bustle and have a restful experience. Most are surprised and amazed at how bright the stars appear at night, with little ground clutter from city lights to dim their beauty. They sparkle against the inky sky, punctuated by the pellucid glow of the moon.

Finding constellations and planets and enjoying the immense stellar spread of the Milky Way above can be a spiritual experience during an evening around the firepit—the low flames and embers the only illumination for miles. To think that the light of many of these heavenly bodies has traveled millions of light-years to reach our eyes, suspended in space and held there by their Creator for his pleasure—and ours—is breathtaking. It causes us to feel so small, yet big at the same time: small because of our scale relative to the vastness of the universe, and big because our heavenly Father is mindful of us—his children whom he loves, values, treasures, and delights in.

The psalmist David expresses this dichotomy of emotions so beautifully:

When I look at the night sky and see the work of
    your fingers—
  the moon and the stars you set in place—
what are mere mortals that you should think about them,
  human beings that you should care for them?
Yet you made them only a little lower than God
  and crowned them with glory and honor.
You gave them charge of everything you made,
  putting all things under their authority—
the flocks and the herds
  and all the wild animals,
the birds in the sky, the fish in the sea,
  and everything that swims the ocean currents.
O LORD, our Lord, your majestic name fills the earth!
PSALM 8:3-9

God is not only mindful of us—but also *cares* for us, *crowns us
with glory*, and *honors* us by entrusting us with *authority* over all living things he's created. Think of it: This awesome Creator, whose
"majestic name fills the earth," has made us capable stewards of this
spinning orb on which he's placed us. Nature provides our food,
shelter, clothing, and opportunities for relishing its beauty, and in
return each of us has a vital role in protecting God's domain for those
who will come after us. We can do this in a way that brings him
glory and furthers his purposes in the world. A starry, starry night is
a wonderful reminder of these important truths.

Consider how you can bring glory to God in the way you live by being more mindful of caring for his creation. Thank him for being mindful of you in his vast universe.

Horse Fuzz

ON THE FARM, perhaps more than anywhere else, you don't need to consult a calendar to know when winter is approaching. Geese fly overheard in V formation on their journey south, the persimmon tree ripens and gives the sweet gift of its fruit, and the mountain forests are covered in vibrant fall hues. There is a chill in the air.

What's especially amazing is that Rooster Cogburn is already growing his fuzzy winter coat in earnest. Do the colder temperatures cause this? It may seem like the most logical answer, but the real trigger is the diminishing daylight. As the fall days get shorter, Rooster Cogburn's body produces more of the hormone melatonin, prompting the additional coat growth. When daylight increases again in the spring, his melatonin production drops, and he sheds his coat.

Rooster's cousin, located a few hundred miles south of Fodderstack Farm, has a thinner coat. Longer sunlight in this warmer region means the horses there produce less melatonin and have lighter winter coats. Northern horses begin to grow their winter coats as early as August or September, well ahead of the cold.

Rooster and his cousin each naturally grow the exact coats they need. How awesome is our Creator to make these creatures' bodies with the innate ability to protect themselves? As the seasons and temperatures change, God prepares them for survival with the provision he's made.

For us, there are seasons of life as well. It's inevitable we will all face difficult stretches of time when it seems our light has faded and we're in need of extra spiritual protection. Even now we may be facing storms from all directions that threaten to overcome our well-being.

How encouraging to know that God has equipped us ahead of time with everything we need to withstand them. He knows when the rough seasons are coming and has thought about exactly how much spiritual melatonin we will need to make it through. He goes before us and does not leave us on our own—naked, afraid, and cold. He's promised his presence and given us his Word to speak comforting truth to us when we need it the most. We are also surrounded by the body of Christ for encouragement and care.

Just like with Rooster Cogburn, these provisions from our God cover us like a warm and fuzzy coat in winter—until the spring comes again.

Do not be afraid or discouraged, for the LORD will personally go ahead of you. He will be with you; he will neither fail you nor abandon you.

DEUTERONOMY 31:8

Reflect on periods of your life when God provided for you amid dark, cold, and stormy times. Write a prayer thanking him for his faithfulness.

Water Trough

THE BACK PASTURE at Fodderstack Farm is home to a large oblong water trough. Drew and Renee usually fill it only about a quarter full since it's a beast to empty when fresh water is needed. Renee was filling it one day when she lost her focus and let the water rise more than halfway. When it was time to dump and refill the trough, she couldn't ask Drew to help since he was sick with a cold. Renee tried rocking it, hoping the water would slosh over the opposite rim. Not so. She gave all her strength in a final push, but it was not enough. She lost her balance and fell into the trough, hitting her shoulder on the rim. While she lay there in the cold water, experiencing enormous pain, the sheep wandered up to look at the strange sight. Renee's resulting bone bruise lasted for months.

Most of us view self-sufficiency as a positive attribute, a key to success. Rugged individualism is a quintessential American characteristic; we take pride in relying on our own strength to accomplish what we set out to do. As the saying goes, "If you want a thing done well, do it yourself." But is this always the best approach to every life situation? What if it involves our eternal destiny?

In the Kingdom of God, there are many countercultural truths, and the central one is that we *can't* make it on our own. We must realize our limitations, and most important, that we can't forgive our own sins. Reliance on our good works will not secure our entrance into heaven but will ultimately end in death. We need transforming faith in the Cross of Christ, where he shed his blood to erase our sins, giving us eternal life. And we need the Holy Spirit's power to repent and live for God.

We hear a lot about "empowerment," the idea that it's possible for individuals to garner enough power to change themselves and the world. This humanistic perspective says that if we free our minds and believe in ourselves and our good ideas, we can do great things. But Philippians 4:13 says, "I can do everything through *Christ*, who gives me strength," and Jesus says in John 8:31-32, "You are truly my disciples if you remain faithful to *my* teachings. And you will know the truth, and the truth will set you free" (emphasis added). We must come to believe that we are utterly reliant on God and not our own power. It's God's strength and truth that we must lean into—not only for salvation but also for daily life.

Renee's water trough story is a great reminder that we must embrace our need for the God who created us.

In what ways are you relying on yourself instead of God?
Meditate on Ephesians 3:20: "Now all glory to God,
who is able, through his mighty power at work within us,
to accomplish infinitely more than we might ask or think."

Snowflake Wonder

SNOWFALL AT FODDERSTACK FARM isn't a regular occurrence, with annual amounts at only eight inches. But when it does snow, it's breathtaking, covering the mountains, pastures, animals, and buildings in a lovely glistening white—a picture belonging on a postcard.

This fresh blanketing of snow makes everything look so clean and pure. It reminds us how God forgives and cleanses us when we draw near to him: "Though your sins are like scarlet, I will make them as white as snow" (Isaiah 1:18). In that covering of white that stretches as far as the eye can see, it boggles the mind to think that every snowflake is different.

Have you ever wondered how a snowflake is made? It begins to form when a cold water droplet freezes onto a tiny pollen or dust particle in the sky, making an ice crystal. As it falls to the ground, water vapor freezes onto the primary crystal, building new crystals and creating the hexagonal structure of the snowflake.

Because individual snowflakes follow slightly different paths from the sky to the ground, they experience different atmospheric conditions along the way. The unique, intricate patterns of the six arms they grow are based on temperature and humidity. Their shapes can appear like prisms, needles, and lace; each one is exquisite in its design.

Snow is not only beautiful; it's also necessary. It has an important purpose. Isaiah 55:10 says, "The rain and snow come down from the heavens and stay on the ground to water the earth. They cause the grain to grow, producing seed for the farmer and bread for the hungry."

It all starts with a tiny, ordinary particle of pollen or dust—so small that it is nearly invisible. Together, the individual flakes combine to make a beautiful and useful snowfall.

There are important lessons we can learn from snowflakes: God takes the tiniest inconsequential particle of debris to create a thing that, on its own or combined with others of its kind, takes our breath away in its beauty. He can make something insignificant into something useful, watering the earth.

If God can do this with a dust particle, how much more can he use you, whom he also created so fearfully and wonderfully from the dust? We each follow a different path through life that shapes and forms us—unique and beautiful in our design. Together with like-minded brothers and sisters, unified in purpose, we can blanket the world with the message of God's forgiving, saving, cleansing, nourishing power—like a fresh snowfall.

He performs wonders that cannot be fathomed,
    miracles that cannot be counted.

JOB 5:9, NIV

180

We can learn from something as simple yet complex as a snow-flake. How can you apply this miraculous lesson to your life? How has God uniquely formed and shaped you? How can you best unite with fellow believers to accomplish God's purposes?

Less Waste, More Joy

Appreciating the beauty and wonder of the earth inspires us to preserve and care for it. What can you do to keep God's creation as healthy as possible? One thing we can all do is reduce the amount of trash we create. Our modern life, filled with conveniences and prepackaged materials, inevitably creates a lot of garbage.

Although a portion of our trash is recycled, the rest ends up in landfills, not only creating an environmental issue but also costing us time and money spent managing, bagging, hauling, transporting, and disposing of it all. Take a small step in the right direction by going back to the basics and looking for ways to throw less out. The following are some ideas to consider.

- Be mindful of what you buy. Choose products with minimal or recyclable packaging. Substitute paper products with cloth: Napkins, paper towels, tissue, and cotton pads can be replaced with washable cloth. Select ceramic, wooden, silicone, or natural rubber children's toys and dishes. Bring your own travel coffee mug to the coffee shop or drive-through. Invest in a reusable water bottle. Request eco-friendly or "frustration-free" packaging when ordering deliveries.
- Reduce use of plastic. Avoid plastic shopping bags by bringing your own, choosing paper bags instead, or investing in reusable cloth totes; avoid produce bags by keeping produce loose in your grocery cart, or purchase a set of reusable mesh drawstring bags. When ordering from restaurants, ask that plastic utensils and straws not be included with your order.

Search online for recipes to make your own cleaning products, and use reusable spray bottles. Buy food in bulk (bring your own containers to the store), and store it in metal or glass jars.

- Recycle. Many communities have a recycling program for paper, cardboard, cans, glass, and common plastics. Recycling outlets are also available for nonrecyclable plastics, Styrofoam, electronics, cassette tapes/CDs, etc.—you will need to research what is available in your area and drop off the items there yourself. Go a step further and offer to be the neighborhood collection point for others' hard-to-recycle items since you will be making a drop-off anyway.

- Compost. As we eat healthier and incorporate more fresh produce into our diets, we generate more food waste. Vegetable scraps are a great starter kit for making your own vegetable stock, or if you have farm animals, you can add the scraps to their feed. Food scraps will also decompose, adding nutrients to your flower beds or garden.

The verdict is in: A few new habits and choices can help you create less waste, enjoy a more natural and healthy lifestyle, save money, and take joy in knowing you're caring for the planet.

Notes

FARM HOSPITALITY

1. "The overwhelming feeling and theme of the barn house is *hospitality*, which one source defines as 'the friendly and generous reception and entertainment of guests, visitors, or strangers.'" See Lexico (online), s.v. "hospitality," accessed August 5, 2020, https://www.lexico.com/en/definition/hospitality.

2. "The word comes from the Latin *hospes*, meaning 'sojourner, visitor, guest . . . friend.'" See Carlton T. Lewis, *An Elementary Latin Dictionary*, 3rd ed. (New York: American Book Company, 1918), 371, https://www.google.com/books/edition /An_Elementary_Latin_Dictionary/JoRI2BxODJMC?hl=en&gbpv=1&dq=%E2 %80%9Csojourner,+visitor,+guest%22&pg=PA371&printsec=frontcover.

3. "It's also related to the words *host, hospice, hostel*, and *hotel*." See "Had a Long Day of Travel? Check into a Hospital," Merriam-Webster.com, accessed August 5, 2020, https://www.merriam-webster.com/words-at-play/word-history-hospital-hostel-hotel -hospice.

BE STILL

1. "Dear Lord, be with me today. Listen to my confusion and help me know how to live it. I don't know the words. I don't know the way. Show me the way. You are a quiet God. Help me to listen to your voice in a noisy world. I want to be with you. I know you are peace. I know you are joy. Help me to be a peaceful and joyful person. These are the fruits of living close to you. Bring me close to you, dear Lord. Amen." Henri J. M. Nouwen, *Following Jesus: Finding Our Way Home in an Age of Anxiety* (New York: Convergent Books, 2019), 14–15.

MAJESTIC MOUNTAINS

1. "Besides being enchanting to look at, mountains create spectacular waterfalls, and this area of the Pisgah National Forest, known as the 'Land of Waterfalls,' is home

to more than 250 of them." See "Land of Waterfalls: 250+ Cascades Near Brevard," Visit North Carolina, accessed November 17, 2020, https://www.worldatlas.com /articles/how-much-of-the-world-s-land-mass-is-mountainous.html.

2. "More than half of the world's population depends on mountains for water." See "Mountains Matter," The Mountain Institute, accessed November 17, 2020, https://mountain.org/why-mountains/.

MASTER GARDENER

1. "God often uses circumstances to transplant His people into the place He wants them to be." Jill Briscoe, quoted at Telling the Truth with Stuart, Jill, and Pete Briscoe, Facebook meme, February 18, 2019, https://www.facebook.com/tellingthetruth /photos/sometimes-its-hard-to-understand-what-god-is-doing-in-us-especially -when-circums/10156882978309774.

2. "Sometimes when you're in a dark place you think you've been buried when you've actually been planted." Christine Caine, quoted in *365 Devotions for a Thankful Heart* (Grand Rapids, MI: Zondervan, 2018), July 11.

RAISING CHICKENS

1. "A tissue analysis from T. rex dinosaur bones excavated in Montana in 2003 indicates the dinosaur shares more genetic material with domestic chickens than with reptiles." See John Noble Wilford, "Tests Confirm T. Rex Kinship with Birds," *New York Times*, April 25, 2008, https://www.nytimes.com/2008/04/25/science/25dino .html?_r=1&auth=login-facebook&ei=5090&emc=rss&en=26facf8338b0b4f7 &ex=1366776000&oref=slogin&partner=rssuserland.

2. "Domestic chickens may have come to the Americas from Polynesia at least one hundred years before Columbus. At an archaeological site in coastal Chile, excavators found chicken bones dated between AD 1304 and 1424." See Heather Whipps, "Chicken Bones Suggest Polynesians Found Americas before Columbus," Live Science, June 4 2007, https://www .livescience.com/1567-chicken-bones-suggest-polynesians-americas-columbus.html.

3. "Chickens arrived in North America from Europe in the sixteenth and seventeenth centuries when Dutch and Portuguese slave traders brought them over from Africa; chicken remains similar to those found in Spain have also been found in Haiti and Florida." See Kristina Killgrove, "Ancient DNA Explains How Chickens Got to the Americas," *Forbes*, November 23, 2017, https://www.forbes.com/sites/kristinakillgrove /2017/11/23/ancient-dna-explains-how-chickens-got-to-the-americas/?sh=38c5d21156db.

CROW ANGELS

1. "As humans, we also face 'many dangers, toils, and snares.'" John Newton, "Amazing Grace," 1779.

NOTES

OLD-TIME LAUNDRY

1. "1858: The first rotary washing machine was patented, though it was hand-cranked and still a lot of work to use." See "U.S. Census Bureau Daily Feature for October 26: Washing Machines," Cision PR Newswire, October 26, 2016, https://www.prnewswire .com/news-releases/us-census-bureau-daily-feature-for-october-26-washing-machines -300343533.html.
2. "1908: The first electric washer was developed." See "U.S. Census Bureau Daily Feature for October 26."
3. "1930s: The first fully automatic washer with a spin cycle was marketed." See "U.S. Census Bureau Daily Feature for October 26."
4. "In 2016, more than 85% of all US households had a washing machine." See "U.S. Census Bureau Daily Feature for October 26."
5. "In 1955, only 10% of US households had a clothes dryer." See Margaret Morris, "The History of the Clothes Dryer," The Classroom, updated July 21, 2017, https:// www.theclassroom.com/the-history-of-the-clothes-dryer-13410374.html.
6. "This figure rose to nearly 80% by 2009." See "Distribution of Households with Clothes Dryers in the U.S. in 2009, by Energy Source," Statista, accessed January 11, 2021, https://www.statista.com/statistics/220466/household-penetration-of-clothes -dryers-by-energy-source-in-the-us/.
7. "In 2006, 83% of Americans considered the clothes dryer a necessary appliance. By 2010, the percentage had dropped to 59% according to a survey by the Pew Research Center." See "5 Reasons to Ditch your Dryer," Green America, accessed January 11, 2021, https://www.greenamerica.org/green-living/ditch-your-dryer.

ON HELPLESSNESS

1. "Be not anxious because of your helplessness. Above all, do not let it prevent you from praying. Helplessness is the real secret and the impelling power of prayer. You should therefore rather try to thank God for the feeling of helplessness which He has given you. It is one of the greatest gifts which God can impart to us. For it is only when we are helpless that we open our hearts to Jesus and let Him help us in our distress, according to His grace and mercy." O. Hallesby, *Prayer*, trans. Clarence J. Carlsen (Minneapolis: Augsburg, 1994), 23.

BLUEGRASS BEAUTY

1. "Stepping into the Blue Ridge is like stepping into a folk song about a bygone era of bygone values and ways, and the breezes bear the songs of ghostly fiddles and the forgotten people who made them talk and who played a fundamental and lasting role in the development of American culture." Bob Sihler, "Blue Ridge Parkway," SummitPost.org, accessed November 20, 2020, https://www.summitpost.org/blue-ridge-parkway/239448.

2. "There is no complete spiritual life without music, for the human soul has regions which can be illuminated only by music." Zoltán Kodály, quoted in Helga Szabo, *The Kodály Concept of Music Education* (London: Boosey & Hawkes, 1969), http://www .kodaly.org.au/assets/Australian_Kodaly_Journal_2009.pdf.

THE TREASURE OF TIME

1. "Did I offer peace today? Did I bring a smile to someone's face? Did I say words of healing? Did I let go of my anger and resentments? Did I forgive? Did I love? These are the real questions! I must trust that the little bit of love that I sow now will bear many fruits, here in this world and in the life to come." Henri Nouwen, *Sabbatical Journey* (New York: Crossroad, 1998), 61.

FARM-TO-TABLE

1. "It means it came *directly* from the farm and wasn't shipped, processed, frozen, held in a distributor's warehouse, or stocked in a grocery store on its way to your table." See Molly Watson, "The Meaning of Farm-to-Table," The Spruce: Eats, September 27, 2019, https://www.thespruceeats.com/farm-to-table-2216574.

2. "There are also economic and environmental benefits, including less air pollution and use of pesticides, as well as healthier soil, due in part to crop rotation and other methods used by many small farms. Buying local food also creates local jobs, positively impacting the community. Your own pocketbook will benefit, too, if you adjust your menus to take advantage of seasonal, readily available meat and produce. "See Lisa Drayer, "Eat Farm-to(-Your-Kitchen)-Table Because It's Good for You and the Earth; Here's How," CNN, August 2, 2018, https://www.cnn.com/2018/08/02 /health/farm-to-table-food-drayer/index.html.

3. "Many farms host fundraisers or plan special dining experiences that allow people to enjoy literal farm-to-table meals in a natural setting, often served family style." See Dawn Pick Benson, "The Farm to Table Dinner," Home Is Here, July 23, 2014, https://www.thespruceeats.com/farm-to-table-2216574http://homeishere.furniture row.com/farm-to-table-dinner/.

4. "Be careful, however, about farm-to-table claims, as there's no standard criteria or regulated definition of the term." See Emma Diab, "What It Really Means When a Restaurant Is 'Farm-to-Table,'" Thrillist, March 24, 2016, https://www.thrillist.com /eat/nation/what-it-really-means-when-a-restaurant-is-farm-to-table.

BREAD 'N' BUTTER

1. "Researchers have identified more than twenty compounds that contribute to the aroma of baked goods, the most common scents being milky, buttery, and malty." See "Why Does Baking Bread Smell So Good?" Modernist Cuisine, August 22, 2018,

https://modernistcuisine.com/mc/why-does-baking-bread-smell-so-good/; "Aroma Chemistry: The Aroma of Fresh-Baked Bread," Ci/Compound Interest, accessed January 7, 2021, https://i0.wp.com/www.compoundchem.com/wp-content/uploads /2016/01/Aroma-Chemistry-%E2%80%93-Fresh-Baked-Bread.png?ssl=1; and Conor Pope, "Why Do We Love the Smell of Bread? UCD Scientists Find the Answer," Irish Times, September 8, 2017, https://www.irishtimes.com/life-and-style/food-and-drink /why-do-we-love-the-smell-of-bread-ucd-scientists-find-the-answer-1.3213506\.

2. "A 2017 Irish study found that 89 percent of people said the smell of bread made them happy, and a French study found the aroma of freshly baked bread can not only put you in a better mood but also make you kinder toward others." See Pope, "Why Do We Love the Smell of Bread?" and Sarah Medina, "The Smell of Fresh Baked Bread Makes Us Kinder to Strangers, Says New Study," HuffPost, updated November 5, 2012, https://www.huffpost.com/entry/the-smell-of-fresh-baked-_n_2058480.

3. "Flavored butter will last in your refrigerator up to a few weeks, or longer in the freezer." See Auroris, "Homemade Flavoured Butters," Instructables Cooking, accessed January 7, 2021, https://www.instructables.com/id/Homemade-Flavoured-Butters/?linkId =65990839.

THE SHEPHERD'S PSALM

1. "David himself had been a keeper of the sheep and understood both the needs of the sheep and the many cares of a shepherd. He compares himself to a creature weak, defenseless, and foolish, and he takes God to be his Provider, Preserver, Director and, indeed, his everything." Charles Spurgeon, *Spurgeon's Daily Treasures in the Psalms: Selections from the Classic Treasury of David*, ed. Roger Campbell (Grand Rapids, MI: Kregel, 2013), February 17, "My Shepherd."

CANINE SUNBATHERS

1. "We draw people to Christ not . . . by telling them how wrong they are and how right we are, but by showing them a light that is so lovely that they want with all their hearts to know the source of it." Madeleine L'Engle, quoted in Sarah Arthur's, *A Light So Lovely: The Spiritual Legacy of Madeleine L'Engle* (Grand Rapids, MI: Zondervan, 2018), 15.

BEEKEEPING

1. "It's estimated that up to 125,000 people in the US now keep bees, both as a hobby and commercially." See "Bees," Agricultural Marketing Resource Center, revised May 2020, https://www.agmrc.org/commodities-products/livestock/bees-profile#:~:text =In%20the%20United%20States%20there,million%20pounds%20of%20raw%20 honey.

2.   "Ancient Egyptians practiced beekeeping using hives made by mixing straw and clay."
     See Jimmy Stamp, "The Secret to the Modern Beehive Is a One-Centimeter Air
     Gap," *Smithsonian Magazine*, September 6, 2013, https://www.smithsonianmag.com
     /arts-culture/the-secret-to-the-modern-beehive-is-a-one-centimeter-air-gap-4427011/.
3.   "Artificial hives with varying designs have been used over the centuries. Today's most
     common structure originates from Lorenzo Langstroth, a Massachusetts school
     principal who patented his design in 1852." See Stamp, "The Secret to the Modern
     Beehive."
4.   "The easiest way to start your colony is to buy bees from a local beekeeping
     organization." See "Beekeeping 101: Where to Get Honey Bees," *The Old Farmer's
     Almanac*, April 29, 2020, https://www.almanac.com/beekeeping-101-where-get-bees.

CRAFT THERAPY

1.   "Taking a cue from how occupational therapists used activities such as basket weaving
     and knitting to help veterans of World Wars I and II recover from shell shock, crafts
     are now used to treat post-traumatic stress disorder (PTSD), depression, chronic
     fatigue syndrome, and anorexia. Researchers continue to seek understanding of how
     craft activities benefit body and mind." See Susan Luckman, "How Doing Craft Is
     Good for Our Health," Inner Self, accessed January 17, 2021, https://innerself.com
     /content/living/leisure-and-creativity/17499-how-doing-craft-is-good-for-our-health
     .html.

About Terri Kraus

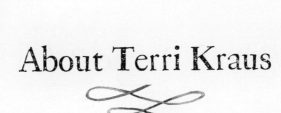

TERRI KRAUS is the author of three published novels—the Project Restoration series—and has coauthored ten published novels with her husband, Jim.

A graduate of the University of Illinois School of Art and Design, Terri began her writing career after twenty years as a professional interior designer and college teacher. She served as president of Redbud Writers Guild for more than six years and has hosted a book club for twenty-four years.

Terri's ministry heart is for women: She has served on the board of directors for the Re:new Project, which employs female refugees, and as the women's ministries director at her church. She also founded a nonprofit coalition to raise awareness about human trafficking.

Terri loves to cook Italian family recipes and has enjoyed extensive travel in the United States and abroad with her family. She and Jim have one married son—Elliot—and live in Bluffton, South Carolina, with their miniature schnauzer, Sadie.

Visit Terri's website at terrikraus.com.

About Renee Baker

AFTER A SEVEN-YEAR CAREER in marketing, where she met her husband, Drew, Renee Baker devoted herself to raising her two daughters in suburban Chicago.

In 2008, after becoming empty nesters, the couple moved to the mountains of western North Carolina. Discovery of an abandoned farm with amazing potential and a beautiful view of Fodderstack Mountain led to a year of renovation. Animals filled up the new nest, followed by guests in the barn house, which Renee developed into a vacation rental property.

The supply of wool from the sheep grew, so Renee learned the craft of hand-processing wool at the John C. Campbell Folk School. Working to hone her skills added friends and more creative challenges. Sharpening her knowledge of photography with teachers in the United States and Scotland is Renee's latest adventure.

Visit her website at FodderstackFarm.com.